To My Mother

From your d...

Merry Christmas
2009

PILOTS

PILOTS

A SPECIAL BREED

AUTHOR

BOBBY K. TERRY SR. CFII

CO/AUTHOR

BOBBY K. TERRY JR. M.S.

Photographic Journalists

Keely Anders

Sheila Anders

Kristin Burgin

Deborah Cole

To order additional copies of this book, contact:
Xlibris Corporation
1-888-795-4274
www.Xlibris.com
Orders@Xlibris.com
40571

CONTENTS

Contact Information:

Website *www.tiptopwebsite.com/bobbykterrycfii*

Correspondence may be directed to:

Terry Enterprises Idabel Airport

2920 Airport Road

Idabel, Oklahoma 74745

Telephone: 580-286-3538 and 903-782-9778 (8AM-5PM 7 days/ week)

Fax: 580-208-2951
bkt@beloemail.com

FREE FALLING

Climbing into the heavens I wonder where you live.
I look at the clouds and I wonder if they are your pillows at night.
I wonder if little angels playfully jump from one to another,
Knocking the rain out as they go.
Finally at 11,000 feet into the sky,
So cool up here, it's time to jump.
My heart is pounding in my throat,
I say a prayer to you,
If I die . . .
The rush flows through like nothing I have ever known,
Suddenly my body is not my own.
Everything is surreal, I can't describe what I feel.
I have the excitement, the fear
The disbelief that I am even here.
As I free fall I somehow know that you are near,
Protecting me in my childish adventure.
I know that if I die I'd free fall into your arms.
There I would lie in a peace I could never describe

Teri R. Mackie

ABOUT THE AUTHORS

Bobby K. Terry Sr. is a retired Army Officer and the owner and senior instructor of Terry's Aviation Flying Service Idabel, OK.

His qualifications include:

Bachelor's degree from New Mexico State University

Bachelor's degree from The University of Texas

Teacher Certification K-12 Texas A & M

CFI

CFII

Gold Seal Flight Instructor

Holder of 6 distinct ratings to include:

1. Private
2. Instrument
3. Commercial
4. Multiple engine
5. Helicopter
6. Airline Transport Pilot

Bobby K. Terry Jr. served as a sergeant in the United States Marine Corp from 1986 until 1993. His last assignment was as a marksmanship instructor from 1991 until 1993. He is currently employed by Dr. John Hansen Executive Director of the Ingenuity Center located at The University of Texas Tyler Campus. His accomplishments are as follows:

Bachelors and Masters Degrees from Stephen F. Austin State University Nacogdoches, Texas.

Madison's Who's Who for Professionals

The National Deans List

The Chancellors List

National Scholars Honor Society

Alpha Chi National Honor Society

Phi Upsilon Omnicron

Epsilon Pi Tau

ACKNOWLEDGEMENTS

Aviation will always be the second greatest love of my life, as my wife Jeanice and my extended family will always be number one in my life time. Without the love, support and encouragement I could not have accomplished all of my goals in life. In parting I would like to share my philosophy concerning life:

Always have spiritual values in your heart and your loved ones on your mind!

Best of luck in your flying endeavors, Bobby K. Terry Sr.

I would like to thank my mentor Dr. Mark Miller for teaching me everything I know about higher education.

Bobby K. Terry Jr.

INTRODUCTION

I would like to begin by thanking everyone for picking up a copy of this book entitled, "Pilots a Special Breed". Pilots are a very special breed, they love adventure, they are very goal oriented and most of all they love a challenge. I believe that is why I admire and relate so well to pilots and everyone in the flying community. I was born during the Second World War in 1935; my birth place was Harris Oklahoma. Horace Greeley knew exactly what he was talking about when he told young men to head west! Life in Oklahoma was very hard during the 1930's and 1940's.

My parents Lena & Colvin Terry were hard working cotton farmers. My dad died of pneumonia in 1940. I was the youngest of six children, I had 2 brothers Rowland and Alfred and my 3 sisters Jo, Imajene and Dorothy. Once my dad passed away a great deal of responsibility fell upon my 5 siblings. By age 9 I could operate a tractor and even chop some small pieces of wood. Life in Oklahoma in those days was hand to mouth as I remember living in a farm-house that was lit by carosnie lamps and heated by a wooden stove, water came from a well and we had an outhouse in the back.

It is a long way from the modern living we take for granted today, massive airports in every major city, luxury airlines like the 777 and of course the popular E-ticket. My first memory of aviation was watching the bi-planes dust the crops. Charles Lindberg made the first solo flight across the Atlantic in 1927 and Amelia Earhart vanished 2 years after my birth in 1937. Even in Oklahoma everyone knew their names and they were famous. When I turned fourteen my mother sold the farm and we moved to the small town of Idabel, Oklahoma. I was enrolled at Idabel Grey High in 1950.

At that time Chuck Yeager was a National hero and he became my boyhood idol. I dreamed of breaking the speed barrier just like him and becoming a great aviator maybe even a jet fighter pilot. I was fortunate enough to play all sports in high school I made the varsity football team as a true freshman and played defensive end throughout high school. I was scouted by numerous colleges for scholarships opportunities. I even meet Bud Wilkinson, the famous University of Oklahoma coach as a junior. I was given a football scholarship to attend Eastern Oklahoma A & M.

After a career ending injury I decided to transfer to New Mexico State University and pursue an accounting degree with the ambition of becoming a CPA. At this point in my life I decided to join the United States Army. For the next twenty four years I would be fortunate enough to have a very successful career. I started out as a private and eventually achieved the rank of Sergeant First Class; my next promotion was to be commissioned as a second lieutenant. I would be promoted two more times during my long career. I would serve as a combat engineer on both active and reserve assignments. My two greatest achievements personally, were coaching all army sports twice and spending a tour as a combat engineer instructor at Fort Belvoir, Virginia.

My sister Dorothy and her husband Harold owned and operated a large welding business in Farmington, New Mexico. After graduation I went to my sisters to help teach her and my brother-in-law the best way to keep accurate financial records and assist in inventory control and income tax. At this time I had some free time and I spent it all studying aviation textbooks and reading about Manfred von Richtofen the famous "Red Barron", Arthur Roy Brown, James Doolittle, and Orville and Wilbert Wright.

While living in Farmington, I read a newspaper want ad that caught my attention and sparked my interest, "Pilots needed to fly oil field workers to various locations in the four corners to include New Mexico, Arizona, Colorado and Utah". Little did I know at the time, this want-ad would change my life forever! For the first time in my young life I realized that opportunities existed in aviation right here in this small community that was built by oil and gas revenue.

In February 1964, I went to see the Cessna Airplane dealer located at San Juan County Airport. The salesman introduced me to an instructor who was a commercial pilot and a CFII. Besides teaching flying lessons he worked as a pilot for a local oil company and flew employees and executives throughout the 4 corners. We discussed the want ad I had read in the paper and he told me I would have to acquire a series of licenses to achieve this type of employment, but he could help me reach my goal.

Forty years later I have accomplished everything I have set out to do in the world of aviation. There are many times that I have been approached by young men who had the same aspirations as I did in 1967. That is the great thing about my chosen profession not only have I been able to help people accomplish their goals just like my instructor did for me in the 60's, it has been a family affair. My wife Jeanice has been the foundation of my career without her love and support I would never have achieved my goal to become a Gold Seal Flight Instructor. I would like to discuss my views on goal setting and what they can do for the aspiring pilot.

GOALS

Bill boards are popular in America for a reason; they are large, colorful and make for good advertisement as people see them on a regular basis. This leads to retention people just remember billboards. I recommend that all pilots no matter what the level go to an office supply store and purchase a 12 month calendar that has all the months visible. These usually are 2 feet by 3 feet in size. Hang the calendar somewhere obvious where you can see it on a regular basis, mine is hanging in the kitchen. The Dry Erase kinds are the best and it is worth the investment. Use it ONLY for aviation planning, make a commitment to yourself by planning your flying as far in advance as you can.

It has been said, "If you leave the dock without a map you may never get where you want to go!" I can guarantee you one thing, you will get lost and it will happen very quickly! Setting proper goals is your map and only you know where you want to go. I have my own philosophy when it comes to setting goals when I decided to play college football at a young age I learned the value of goal setting. I have tried to set goals in all parts of my life, family, church, financial and of course in my career. I personally believe it is a five part process. I will explain it and given a very typical example of a well planned goal that can be accomplished by just about anyone who is motivated and dedicated enough.

THE SPECIFICS OF MAKING YOUR
GOALS A REALITY

1st   Goals should be written down and posted where than can be seen on a daily basis. For example next to the computer on a dresser or like mine I post them on my refrigerator.

2nd   Goals must be realistic & specific.

3rd   They must have suspense dates.

4th   They must be flexible anticipate problems; have solutions in mind.

5th   Must be measurable.

Good Example:

1st   Goals will be hung on my bathroom mirror so I will see them every morning when I get up.

2nd   I will earn my private pilot's license in 12 months.

3rd   Start January 2008 and finish January 2009.

4th   Problem: I do not have enough financial resources to complete training.
Solution: I will take out a loan
-Or-
Solution: I will change my time frame by six more months until July 2009.

5th   I will have my license in my wallet or purse by January 20th 2009!

It is my opinion part 4 can make or break people's goals. You must always anticipate problems and have solutions ready. The weather is a prime example for me, as an instructor I must be prepared for bad weather. Training does not stop because of weather problems; we can go to the flight simulator or spend extra time preparing for the written exams. If a person is highly motivated, truly dedicated and sticks to a well written plan he or she will reach their goals. The best example is the Olympic athlete that competes every four years. If you ever get discourage with your goals read what they must do to accomplish their goals in winning a coveted Olympic medal!

Next, you need to stay up with the world of aviation, read the current periodicals, training manuals and aviation books. I do my best to stay up with everything as current as possible. Even forty years later I always devote personal time to reading and using the flight simulator from time to time to stay sharp and a step ahead of the other instructors out there, we all know how competitive pilots are! That is one reason I encourage parents to start their children at a young age it teaches discipline, self-control and strengthens the competitive spirit. All of these traits are what this country was founded on, free will and a sense of adventure, as some of our greatest American patriots were aviators.

Like learning an individual sport or a foreign language, the younger one can start the better off they will be. On the flip side of the coin it is never really too late to learn to fly, normally the older person may have to study harder and practice a little more but the rewards and sense of accomplishment are truly priceless. I have witnessed great flying success's at all different ages, and the pictorial part of this book is a testament to that fact! Now, that bring me to the inspirational moment I had for writing this book.

INSPIRATION

I have been fortunate enough to own and operate the Terry Aviation School located in my home town of Idabel Oklahoma. I am very proud of the facilities, the staff members and the quality of instruction we offer on a daily basis. The staff and I cater to people's needs; we train all ages and levels of flying experience. Some times that calls for weekend's nights and even the occasion holiday. But, we all believe that successful training needs no rigid time schedule. We want the student to be comfortable and relaxed with no outside interference or schedule conflict. I have found that a distracted pilot is not a safe pilot and safety takes top priority in flight training. In light of our philosophy at the school I found myself in Idabel on a Saturday in July 2006 accompanied by my wife and great granddaughter Konnor Burgin. We were there to spend the morning with some young pilots who needed weekend ground school because of their employment schedule.

When we were done I began to lock up the school and on my way out I noticed my wife entertaining my great granddaughter playing around with aviation toys. It was one of those Kodak moments and unfortunately I had no camera not even on my cell phone. As we drove back to our home in Paris Texas it really struck me how wonderful a moment that was and there had been many wonderful moments in my forty years I have spent in aviation. But I never had the time to keep a detailed scrap book of all my students and my interactions with them. I also realized after ground school that weekend there are certain bodies of common knowledge all pilots should know and remember.

THE PURPOSE OF THIS BOOK

After the drive home I decided it would be very beneficial for me to leave something behind when I am gone, a legacy for my family and my dedicated students. In 2006 I along with my son, began preparing a manuscript. This book was written to accomplish 2 things for aspiring pilots: First, to motivate them with some great photographs and comments you will find that everyone has their own personal reasons for flying. Second, to impart important common knowledge that I believe all pilots should know in regards to the various certifications they may aspire to achieve. I did not write this as a text book there are no definitions to look up; no test questions to write out or maps to work through. That will all be done in the next book my son and I are currently in the process of writing as this one goes to press. This book is divided into two sections; the first section covers pilot training, different certifications, and cost and flight club basics. The second section is devoted entirely to individual pictures and personal thoughts of, "*Pilots that make up that Special Breed*". I hope you find this book both enjoyable and informative and above all please accept my heartfelt thanks for sharing in my love of flying.

INITIAL FLIGHT TRAINING

As a flight instructor I believe that the two most important character traits a student must possess to be successful are desire and discipline. You must really have the desire to fly to get your license, it is costly and time consuming, but the intangibles far out way the monetary price. The lessons learned from flying can be used for a life time. These lessons can be drawn upon to give a person confidence to succeed in relationships, school and in their careers. One must also be disciplined to study and practice on a regular basis. Without desire and discipline a student will find it difficult to succeed in becoming an accomplished pilot. Before we discuss the specific certifications an aspiring pilot can strive to achieve, it is important to give an overview of what to expect during initial flight training. The student will participate in ground school which is conducted in a classroom environment and the practical application of flight instruction is accomplished in the plane itself. I strongly recommend that everyone interested in flying purchase a copy of *Federal Aviation Regulations/Aeronautical Information Manual* published by ASA. For example, the information concerning ground school training can be found in section 61.105. Prior to attending your first day of school there are some basics for obtaining a student pilot certificate:

1. Be at least 16 years of age.
2. Read speak and understand English.
3. Get a third class medical certificate.

If a person has lofty goals for their aviation career, such as becoming a charter pilot or airline pilot you will need a first or second class medical certificate. In the beginning, I always recommend the third class first because it is good for 24 months and is the least demanding of the physicals to pass. The physician that gives these specific physicals is referred to as an Aviation Medical Examiner.

Normally, on the first day of flight school one will be issued a logbook, a copy of the pilot's operating handbook as well as charts for the local training area a cardboard computer and a plotter. Ground school is designed to reinforce everything you are learning during your practical application training. Dual instruction is when you are flying with your instructor and solo flight is when you take to the skies by yourself. Also ground school prepares you to take and pass the Private Pilot Written Exam. I have found in my career that people who struggle with the written exam lack discipline and attempt to cram everything in at the last minute. That is why you need a calendar to track your studies and practice so you will not be forced to cut corners. Specific long range plans with a contingency has always work out for the best. Everyone has a different situation in life sometimes I recommend students split their time by taking ground school first then doing their practical application second or vice-versa. Once again if the student has the desire and the discipline any one of three ways can be very successful. I have never taken a cookie cutter approach as many large flying schools do.

Dual and solo flight training prepares you to pass the actual flying portion. I prefer to have my students achieve 30 hours of both dual and solo instruction in order to pass the first time around. I encourage my students to log in around 20 hours before them commence with a cross country solo. The student will be evaluated by a Designated Flight Examiner for their practical application flight test. Generally the student will participate in a cross country flight designated by the examiner. The student will prepare a flight plan consisting of:

1. Type of flight plan.
2. Aircraft identification.
3. Aircraft type.
4. True airspeed in knots.
5. Departure point.
6. Departure time.
7. Cruising altitude.
8. Route
9. Destination.
10. Estimated time en route.
11. Remarks.
12. Fuel onboard.
13. Alternate airports.
14. Pilot's information.
15. Number onboard.
16. Color of aircraft.
17. Contact information at destination.

Also the student can expect to be asked general aviation questions by the examiner as well as specifics about navigation, weather and the weight and balance of the plane before and after take-off. When the student passes they will be issued a temporary certificate good for 120 days and the permanent one will come through the postal mail service. This brings us to the different types of certifications a pilot can pursue.

COMMON TYPES OF CERTIFICATIONS

The *FAR/AIM* is a government publication and is very specific and lengthy and rather complicated. Here I have attempted to give the basic requirements for sport pilot, private pilot, and instrument rating requirements, commercial pilot and airline transport pilot.

Sport Pilot Refer to FAR 61.301

The sport pilot concept came into effect in 2004. It is an excellent way to get people involved in flying with limited resources; the greatest advantage for some is that it does not require a medical certificate only a valid driver's license must also be 17 years of age, however there are four restrictions.

- Be able to read, speak, write, and understand English
- Log at least 20 hours of flight time of which at least 15 hours must be dual instruction with a qualified flight instructor, 2 hours must be cross-country dual instruction; 5 hours must be solo flight.
- Fly one solo cross-country over a total distance of 75 or more nautical miles to two different destinations to a full-stop landing. At least one leg of this cross-country must be over a total distance of at least 25 nautical miles.
- Have received 3 hours of dual instruction in the preceding 60 days
- Pass a written test
- Pass a practical test

Recreational Pilot Refer to FAR 61.101

(a) A person who holds a recreational pilot certificate may: (1) Carry no more than one passenger; and (2) Not pay less than the pro rata share of the operating expenses of a flight with a passenger, provided the expenses involve only fuel, oil, airport expenses, or aircraft rental fees. (b) A person who holds a recreational pilot certificate may act as pilot in command of an aircraft on a flight that is within 50 nautical miles from the departure airport, provided that person has: (1) Received ground and flight training for takeoff, departure, arrival, and landing procedures at the departure airport; (2) Received ground and flight training for the area, terrain, and aids to navigation that are in the vicinity of the departure airport; (3) Been found proficient to operate the aircraft at the departure airport and the area within 50 nautical miles from that airport; and (4) Received from an authorized instructor a logbook endorsement, which is carried in the person's possession in the aircraft, that permits flight within 50 nautical miles from the departure airport. (c) A person who holds a recreational pilot certificate may act as pilot in command of an aircraft on a flight that exceeds 50 nautical miles from the departure airport, provided that person has: (1) Received ground and flight training from an authorized instructor on the cross-country training requirements of subpart E of this part that apply to the aircraft rating held; (2) Been found proficient in cross-country flying; and (3) Received from an authorized instructor a logbook endorsement, which is carried on the person's possession in the aircraft, that certifies the person has received and been found proficient in the cross-country training requirements of subpart E of this part that apply to the aircraft rating held. (d) Except as provided in paragraph (h) of this section, a recreational pilot may not act as pilot in command of an aircraft: (1) That is certificated for more than four occupants, with more than one power plant, with a power plant of more than 180 horsepower, or with retractable landing gear. (2) That is classified as a multiengine airplane, powered-lift, glider, airship, or balloon; (3) That is carrying a passenger or property for compensation or hire; (4) For compensation or hire; (5) In furtherance of a business; (6) Between sunset and sunrise; (7) In airspace in which communication with air traffic control is required; (8) At an altitude of more than 10,000 feet MSL or 2,000 feet AGL, whichever is higher; (9) When the flight or surface visibility is less than 3 statute miles; (10) Without visual reference to the surface; (11) On a flight outside the United States; (12) To demonstrate that aircraft in flight to a prospective buyer; (13) That is used in a passenger-carrying airlift and sponsored by a charitable organization; and (14) That is towing any object. (e) A recreational pilot may not act as a pilot flight crewmember on any aircraft for which more than one pilot is required by the type certificate of the aircraft or the regulations under which the flight is conducted, except when: (1) Receiving flight training from a person authorized to provide flight training on board an airship; and (2) No person other than a required flight crewmember is carried on the aircraft. (f) A person who holds a recreational pilot certificate, has logged fewer than 400 flight hours, and has not logged pilot-in-command time in an aircraft within the 180 days preceding the flight shall not act as pilot in command of an aircraft until the pilot receives flight training and a logbook endorsement from an authorized instructor, and the instructor certifies that the person is proficient to act as pilot in command of the aircraft. This requirement can be met in combination with the requirements of §§61.56 and 61.57 of this part, at the discretion of the authorized instructor. (g) A recreational pilot certificate issued under this subpart carries the notation, "Holder does not meet ICAO requirements." (h) For the purpose of obtaining additional certificates or ratings while under the supervision of an authorized instructor, a recreational pilot may fly as the sole occupant of an aircraft: (1) For which the pilot does not hold an appropriate certificate.

Four Restrictions:

1. No more than one passenger.
2. Daytime flight only.
3. No flight above 10,000 feet MSL.
4. No flight in any of the airspace classes that require radio communication classes A, B, C, or D without first obtaining additional instruction and instructor endorsement.

Private Pilot Single Engine Refer to FAR 61.103

The most common student I train is the one who is seeking a private pilot license for a single engine land based aircraft. This pilot cannot fly for compensation but may carry friends and family members and shares the expenses in the flight experience. The private pilot is allowed to fly under the visual flight rules. VFR refers to the rules and regulations that govern procedures for conducting flights under visual condition.

- Be at least 17 years old
- Be able to read, speak, and write the English language
- Obtain at least a third class medical certificate from an Aviation Medical Examiner
- Pass a computerized aeronautical knowledge test
- Accumulate and log a specified amount of training and experience, including the following:

> Under Part 61, experience requirements are specified in Title 14 of the Code of Federal Regulations section 61.109 including at least 40 hours of piloting time including 20 hours of flight with an instructor and 10 hours of solo flight, and other requirements including "cross-country", 10 hours of solo flight time in an airplane, including at least

  - Solo requirements:

    1. 6 hours of solo cross-country time
    2. One solo cross-country flight of at least 150 NM total distance, with full-stop landings at a minimum of three points and with one segment of the flight consisting of a straight-line distance of at least 50 NM between the takeoff and landing locations
    3. Three solo takeoffs and landings to a full stop at an airport with an operating control tower.

  - Night requirements:

    1. 3 hours of night flight training
    2. One cross-country flight of over 100 nautical miles total distance
    3. 10 takeoffs and 10 landings to a full stop (with each landing involving a flight in the traffic pattern) at an airport

  - 3 hours of flight training on the control and maneuvering solely by reference to instruments

- Pass an oral test and flight test administered by an FAA inspector.

Instrument Rating IFR Refer to FAR 61.65

I strongly recommend all of my students to pursue their IFR rating once they get the private pilot certificate and here are the basic requirements:

- 50 hours of cross-country flight time as pilot in command, which can include solo cross-country time as a student pilot. Each cross-country must have a landing at an airport that was at least a straight-line distance of more than 50 NM from the original departure point. Cross-country flight procedures must include at least one cross-country flight that is performed under IFR and consists of a distance of at least 250 NM along airways or ATC-directed routing, an instrument approach at each airport, three different kinds of approaches with the use of navigation systems (ILS, LOC, VOR, ADF, and GPS).
- The candidate also needs a total of 40 hours of actual or simulated instrument time, including 15 hours of instrument flight training from a Flight Instructor certified to teach the instrument rating.
- Up to 20 hours of the instrument training may be accomplished in an approved flight simulator or flight training device if the training was provided by a CFII.
- Within 60 days of the practical test, the candidate needs to log 3 hours of instrument training from a CFII in preparation for the test.
- Receive and log training, as well as obtain a logbook endorsement from your CFII on the following areas of operation: preflight preparation, preflight procedures, air traffic control clearances and procedures, flight by reference to instruments, navigation systems, instrument approach procedures, emergency operations, and post flight procedures.
- Successfully complete the instrument rating practical test (and oral and flight test), as specified in Practical Test Standards (PTS) for the instrument rating, which will be conducted by an FAA designated examiner.

Commercial Pilot Refer to FAR 61.123

- Hold a private pilot certificate and be at least 18 years of age.
- Be able to read, speak, write, and understand the English language
- Accumulate and log a specified amount of training and experience; the following are part of the airplane single-engine land class rating requirements:

  o If training under Part 61, at least 250 hours of piloting time including 20 hours of training with an instructor and 50 hours of solo flight, and other requirements including several "cross-country" flights, i.e. more than

50 nautical miles (93 km) from the departure airport and both solo and instructor-accompanied night flights

- Pass a 100 question aeronautical knowledge test
- Pass an oral test and flight test administered by an FAA inspector.

Airline Transport Pilot Refer to FAR 61.159

You will need at least 1500 hours of flight time and be 23 years of age for an ATP certificate. I have listed minimums for the following four categories:

1. 500 hours of cross-country flight time.
2. 100 hours of night flight time.
3. 75 hours of instrument flight time in actual or simulated instrument conditions.
4. 250 hours of flight time in an airplane as a pilot in command, which includes at least 100 hours cross-country flight time and 25 hours of night flight time.

Flying as a profession

During my formative years which include the 1950's and 1960's there were very few aviation options. At these points in time it was primarily based on a person's socioeconomic status. The greater your family wealth the greater your opportunities were to fly. Granted, it is still a major investment in getting a license but the opportunities for a career are much greater. If you attend a major flight school you will normally pay for surcharges and extras, for example fuel and the rental of the plane at my school all prices are conclusive no hidden costs. The mandatory pilot retirement age was recently extended because of 25% of the pilot work force were in the mandatory retirement range.

I have seen figures that suggest there may be 30,000 commercial pilot job opportunities by the end of the century! I always tell young aspiring pilots that they have two very good options in the millennium they can pursue a warrant officer commission in the Army and train at Fort Rucker to become a helicopter pilot or they can complete their training at a school like mine versus the big aviation schools that have big budgets and huge overhead. I pride myself on maintaining reasonable rates for my students and I do not have hidden costs. I remember in the 1970's I had to make great financial sacrifices to continue my training at a major flight school. These days financing is available and there are a variety of ways to pay which did not exist at that time. If you have the desire I can show you the way to become a successful professional pilot. I always recommend the military first, as it has always been a very big and positive part of my life but, the physical is difficult for many individuals to pass and many fail. As a civilian pilot flat feet will not end a career before it begins!

CONCLUSION

I have had the privilege and good fortunate to have taught 13 different pilots who currently work for major airlines. I understand that their salaries range from $120,000 to over $240,000 depending on their years of experience. In writing this book I could not help but to think of one remarkable young man who used his flying experience to open other doors of opportunity in his life. While I was an adjunct professor at Kilgore Junior College in Kilgore Texas, I meet a young man who wanted to pursue his private pilot license while attending college. He completed his license in 90 days. He was struggling in college but, he excelled in his aviation studies. When he graduated from college he was in the lower half of class. Mark made application to a major oil company in East Texas for a petroleum engineering position. There were approximately 40 other applicants for that position to include many at the top of their class from Texas A & M. Mark was hired for the position over all of the other applicants. I was very excited when he called me to explain he had been hired and that the deciding factor was that he held a private pilot license. They told him a transcript and an interview can only reveal so much about a person, but the fact that he got his license meant to them that he had courage and was not afraid to take risks. At that time the oil business was all about taking risks! I had an opportunity to meet the Governor and Lt. Governor many years ago when I lived in New Mexico. The point is that flying leads to many other opportunities in life and it is an investment that pays dividends forever. Now we shall meet that special breed, the pilots, and read the inspiring stories of why they fly!

PILOTS A *SPECIAL BREED*

Meet every breed right here and find out
how you can join them:

- Private
- Instrument
- Commercial
- Multi Engine
- Helicopter
- Airline Transport
  Pilot

PILOTS: A SPECIAL BREED

FLYING CLUB

In my opinion, after 45 years of flying and after 43 years of being a member of several flying clubs and helping to organize a dozen more, which are still active today (2009) and very successful. Some examples include: Rose City Flying Club of Tyler, Texas (31 years); Texarkana, Arkansas Flying Club (19 years); Wood County Flying Club of Mineola, Texas (21 years); and Lamar McCurtain County flying Club of Idabel, Oklahoma (3 years).

Lamar McCurtain County Flying Club started in January 2006, with 5 members and had 11 full members by December 2008. In 1973, C-172 had an estimated value of $50,000 and started with $38,000 in bank loans. Now the balance is approximately $23,000 with $500 per month payments. The insurance is around $300 per month. Members pay monthly dues of $60 and fly for $50 per hour wet. Members are only required to fly one hour per month. The total is only $110 per month. C-172s rent for $125-$150 per month. To date the club is in the black. Memberships are now worth $2,700 each. In the beginning, they only cost $1,250 each. The dues paid each month are now like a savings account. When a member leaves or transfers out of town, they sell their membership for a profit.

Flying clubs are the best way for a new pilot to keep flying and keep his or her cost to a minimum. The secret to a successful flying club is the president. He keeps the airplanes ready to fly at all times. The members only have to call and schedule the airplane.

All the flying clubs mentioned are successful because their presidents are dedicated to helping other pilots enjoy flying. Lamar McCurtain County Flying Club President Jim Crews of Idabel, Oklahoma is a great example of a dedicated president.

Rose City Flying Club
Tyler, Texas

March 7, 1992

To Whom It May Concern:

Rose City Flying Club started in the summer of 1977 with five members. By 1978 The Club had ten members.

The Club was started with a 1960 Cherokee 180. In the early 80's The Club purchased a 1969 Warrior. In the Mid 80's The Club traded in the Warrior and purchased a 1977 Cherokee Archer. It is fully IFR with a storm scope. In 1989 The Club installed a new Engine in the Archer without asking The members for any additional money.

The Club is in the Black. The Plane is paid for and we have ten members with a waiting list.

In my opinion a Flying Club is the best method for Pilots to fly and help the cost and liability to a minimum.

Any questions or comments please contact.

Sincerely,

Q.D. Harris
President R.C.F.C.
Tyler, Texas

WOOD COUNTY PILOTS ASSOCIATION
FLYING CLUB, INC.
P.O. BOX 847
QUITMAN, TEXAS 75783

February 12, 2007

Attention: Bob Terry

Dear Bob,

Always glad to brag, uh, testify, about the club's success.

History: Club started in the fall of 1986 with a couple of guys and an instructor, Bob Terry, and a 1981 Cessna 152. Initial buy in was $1200.00 for a plane valued about $13000.00. Everyone, myself included, were skeptical at first about sinking money in an aircraft that we did not even know how to fly. Eventually we were persuaded to bite the bullet and we have never had to look back. The club was incorporated in 1967 with 10 members, with monthly dues of $35.00 and time at $22.00 per hour including fuel. We eventually sold the 152 for $22,500 to buy a 172 and that remains our aircraft of choice.

Over the past 20 years we have had close to 100 members, many returning from time to time after a few years off. We like to reserve any shares for sale to returning members but that is not mandatory. We limit shares to 10 members to prevent overcrowding of the schedule and to keep the cost of insurance nominal.

Our most recent membership sold for $4800.00 and one before that for $4500.00. I cannot recall any time in the last several years when we did not have a waiting list. The most recent inquiry was from a gentleman wanting an aircraft so his wife could begin lessons. I told him the going rate and he suggested he would pay a premium if someone would be willing to sell. None have, even though we have a few pilots that seldom fly.

Currently we have almost $13,000.00 in cash and savings, including an investment with Edward D. Jones. We replaced the engine a few years ago with a Lycoming Zero Time engine and close to 800 hours remain and I expect to have adequate funds to pay cash for a replacement engine when the time comes. We spent close to 4 grand this year for new upholstery which knocked a hole in our total cash but with 800 hours remaining we feel confident the funds will be available when the time comes. If for some reason the time comes sooner than expected, we can always get a loan from our local bank, as we have in the past. Most banks relish aircraft loans due to appreciation in value of the aircraft. We are nonprofit and have chosen to keep our dues low as long as reserves are adequate for any emergencies.

In 20 years we have only asked for money over and above dues and flying time one time. We used that extra cash, $100.00 per member, to help purchase and install a GPS radio. Of course, the radio was voted on and approved by all members of the club and still is worth every penny.

I hope this spells out the success of the club adequately. It has been a very good idea for all of us that are involved. If anyone has any questions I am always glad to share my experience with the club. I can be reached most days at 903-763-4356.

Larry C. Hughes
President

PILOTS: A SPECIAL BREED

Emergency Landings!!

Since I have been flying off and on for over 45 years with over 40,000 hours and 38 years of teaching others to fly, I am often asked the question: How many emergency landings have you had to make?

Like many things that happen in life whether negative or positive, I think of the expression "If you want something to happen, just think about it a lot and 90 percent of the time it will happen." I won't dwell on much of the negative things, emergency landings, very long.

In November 1964, I had my first emergency landing. I had just received my private pilot certificate. A friend had asked me to fly his Piper Tri-Pacer around Farmington, New Mexico where I lived, and learn to fly. I left the Farmington Airport heading east. Approximately 10 miles from the airport the mags quit, and I had to land on a dirt oil field road. A mechanic came out and changed the mags. I was able to take off on the dirt road and fly back to Farmington.

My second emergency landing happened in May of 1966. I was flying the same plane over to Aztec, New Mexico to check on a gas well. There was a fire inside the city limits of Aztec. I was circling low to the ground, and then I decided to head back to Farmington. Farmington was about 15 miles away. While circling over the town of Aztec, the engine failed because the plane had run out of fuel. Note: Don't trust any gages on airplanes. Also, don't trust anyone who tells you that the plane is full of fuel. Always check the fuel yourself. I was lucky that the traffic was not on the West side of town. I was able to land on the West side of town on Main Street. The Sheriff Deputy blocked off the street. Someone gave me 5 gallons of gas 87 octane. I was able to fly back to Farmington.

On June 1968, I had my third emergency landing. I was a partner on the 1964 Beach Musketeer. I was active in the Farmington Jaycees. I flew to a meeting in Denver, Colorado. On the flight back to Farmington, just over the mountains out of Denver, my engine started cutting out and a valve was stuck. Therefore, I had to make an emergency landing in a vacant field just north of the Denver Airport. I had almost made it to Columbine Airport. A passenger was with me and on the way down to land in the field he opened the door to jump out. We were still 3,000 feet above the ground. I was able to hold him with my right arm around his neck and land the plane with my left. He forgot he had a seat belt on I probably could not have held him in with the door open. We landed okay in a vacant field, and a van load of hippies took us to the hospital. He was treated for shock. I took him to the main airport and booked him a flight to Santa Fe. I talked to him later on the phone, and he said, "Once is enough for me to fly in a small airplane." I admit after this experience I almost quit flying. A mechanic was able to tow the Beach Musketeer to the Columbine Airport for repairs. I had flown back to Farmington by Frontier Airlines. Weeks went by and the mechanic called me and said the plane was ready. I mailed him a cashier's check for the repairs.

More weeks went by and my wife Clova encouraged me to fly again. She told me to go get the plane before I lost my nerve to fly again. Guess what? I had already lost my nerve to ever fly again. Finally, I decided if I was going to fly again I would try to be the best pilot in the world. In order to do that, I was advised by New Mexico Instructor Garth Greenlee of Farmington, New Mexico to pursue all of the ratings possible including Instructors Rating. He said, "When you teach someone else to fly you will really learn how to be a good pilot." That was what drove me to becoming a flight instructor. I may not have turned out to be the best pilot in the world, but my confidence to fly is "Tops!" In other words, I feel safer driving a small airplane today than driving an automobile.

I will wrap this section up by saying a few other incidents have happened. For example, in the summer of 1988, while teaching Jodi Francis, daughter of Martha and Dwight Francis, to obtain her private pilot certificate, we had to make an emergency landing after taking off twice. We were able to return to the Idabel Airport and land safely. Dwight called me that night and said, "If you don't get your C-150S repaired, my daughter will be looking for a new flight instructor. I did get the repairs done, and he did not find a new instructor. That summer, Jodi received her pilot certificate on her brother. Shawn Francis' 17th birthday. Jodi and Shawn both received their private pilot certificates. Jodi was 18. It was such a pleasure to fly with those kids. It always works this way. When parents fly, they teach their kids to fly at a young age, and they give all the credit to me.

In August 1984, I was teaching several students to fly in Athens, Texas, which is 20 miles west of Tyler, Texas. I was teaching husband and wife Kerry and Connie Stepp to fly. Kerry had his own C-182, and Connie had her own C-172. Kerry received his private pilot certificate before Connie received hers. The Stepps own a ranch and have their own grass landing strip approximately 10 miles north of Athens. Kerry is an electrician and travels all over the state of Texas. Kerry wanted Connie to be able to take off and land from their home to bring him electrical supplies. Connie received her private pilot certificate in her C-172. They are both excellent pilots.

On Sunday afternoon, after church, we met at the Athens Airport. We made several landings in the C-182. We then went to the Stepps' ranch. The wind was out of the South, so we did left down wind because the grass strip is north and south 17 and 35 on attempt to land on 35. They had a lot of trees to go over before touching down on 35. I was going to demonstrate the first landing for Connie, so I knew we had to use full flaps and the slowest air speed possible to land on the strip. As we came over the trees on that hot August afternoon, the C-182 starting sinking too fast. I added full power, and we were still sinking. I did not want to stall the plane as it happened we hit the embankment at the end of the runway with nose gear, and it flipped us upside down and skidded for approximately 200 feet. The shoulder harness was holding both Connie and I in the cockpit. I unfastened her seat belt first, and then she unfastened mine. We were able to crawl out of the wrecked C-182. We walked up to the house and called the Sheriff's Department and FAA. The shoulder straps and God saved our lives that day. We were both taken to the hospital and released without a scratch. It was a miracle. The plane was totaled, but fortunately Kerry had insurance. He was able to replace the C-182 with a C-210.

The next day we were both still in shock but managed to fly her C-172, so we could keep our confidence in flying. I went back to Mineola, Texas and continued to teach more students to fly.

Looking back, I realized that I really owe Connie and Kerry an apology. I hope that they will accept my apology in this book even at this late of a date. I should have told everyone in the aviation community in Athens and Tyler that I was the one flying the plane on that landing not Connie. I did not say she was flying the plane, but I also did not say she was not flying the plane at the time of the accident. I let people assume what they wanted to and that was wrong. I should have cleared the air immediately and told everyone I was the one flying the plane. For that Connie and Kerry, I am sorry. I hope and pray that you have forgiven me even though I do not deserve it.

Later, on July 4, 1985, I was teaching Don Rhodes of Mineola, Texas to fly. Don had 30 hours, and we were flying on his first cross-country flight to Shreveport, Louisiana in a PA28-140 that we had rented from the Mineola Airport. Just southwest of Longview, Texas, our engine quit because of a stuck valve. We were only at 2500 feet, and we saw a hay field just south of our location next to I-20 and HWY 271. I asked Don if he wanted to land the plane in the hay field or talk on the radio to tell Gregg County Tower we were making an emergency landing 10 miles west of the airport. Don said, "Go ahead and land the plane. I'm real good on Radios!" We landed safely and no damage was done to the plane. A cat operator saw us and gave us a ride to the Holiday Inn in Longview, Texas. I called the FAA, but no further action was needed.

Dr. Zimmer and I were flying in July 1989. We were instrument training and lost our electrical power upon return to the Idabel, Oklahoma Airport. Therefore, we could not talk to anyone on the radio. The landing gear was electrical. We tried to pump it down with the hand pump. We were getting low on fuel then. After circling around the airport for several minutes, Dr. Simmer said he was ready to land, and we landed on 17 at the Idabel Airport. Finally, we killed the engine and landed with full flaps on touchdown. It stayed up for a few feet and then the gear collapsed. We landed with the gear up. We walked over to the Terminal Building and called the FAA. They gave us permission to move the plane to a hanger with a tow truck. There is a saying in aviation: "Those that has and those that are going to land with landing gear up."

TOP 100 PILOTS!!!!!

In the 44 years of flying and over 40,000 hours and 35 years of flight instruction I have had the honor and privilege of flying with and associating with some of the greatest people in the world, from teenagers to adults up to the age of 75. My life and the life of my family have been blessed in every way with people from all walks of life in the aviation world.

My experience with teenagers, female and male pilots has been for the most part is that there is really no difference in their ability to fly a plane after 100 hours of flight time. However some pilots just have that natural ability, for lack of better words. They just blow my mind how good they can fly an airplane.

Being the competitive and fun person I believe I am, I couldn't resist publishing my top 100 Pilots. Everyone who appears in this book is very special (A Special Breed!!). If you don't make my list please don't be offended. I'm just having fun with this whole book. This is a retirement gift to myself after 44 years in the aviation business.

Top Female Student Pilots

1. Le'Erin Harmon—Idabel, Oklahoma
   Rachael Meziere—Lavon, Texas

2. Keely Anders—Tyler, Texas

3. Sheila Anders—Tyler, Texas

4. Kristin Burgin—Lone Oak, Texas

5. Debbie Keith—Mt. Vernon, Texas

6. Barbara Todd—Lone Oak, Texas

7. Rebekah Campbell—Paris, Texas

8. Holly Cruise—Greenville, Texas

9. Deborah Cole—Paris, Texas

10. Mary Winters—Tyler, Texas

11. Helen Doughty—Mt. Pleasant, Texas

12. Josie House—Mt. Pleasant, Texas

13. Christy Taylor—Paris, Texas

Top Male Student Pilots

1. Jace Garrison—Ashdown, Arkansas

2. Skyler Burchinal—Paris, Texas

3. Daniel Henry—Honey Grove, Texas

4. Noah Rodgers—Maud, Texas

5. Robert T. Watson—Shreveport, Louisiana

6. Michael Stolba DC—Texarkana, Texas

7. Harold Stone—Mt. Vernon, Texas

8. Kaleb Dyer—Mt. Vernon, Texas

9. Stephen Burgin—Lone Oak, Texas

10. Ruben Sarasosa—Cumby, Texas

11. Richard Doty—Greenville, Texas

12. Kevin Doty—Greenville, Texas

13. Robert Franklin—Greenville, Texas

14. Andy Adams—Tyler, Texas

15. Russell Johnson—Winnsboro, Texas

16. Eddie G. Hill—Atlanta, Texas

17. Courney Hevron—Honey Grove, Texas

Top Female Pilots (Less than 1000 hrs.)

1. Shirley Smith—Idabel, Oklahoma
   Jodi Francis Storey—Idabel, Oklahoma

2. Brandi Richey—Paris, Texas

3. Sharmon Young—Waco, Texas

4. Connie Stepp—Athens, Texas

5. Patsy Pool—Athens, Texas

6. Beth Nix—Mineola, Texas

7. Jane Bateman—Lindale, Texas

8. Gina Nelms—Gilmer, Texas

9. Teresa Maderer—Broken Bow, Oklahoma

10. Cheryl McClendon—Idabel, Oklahoma

Top Female Pilots (Over 1,000 Hours)

1. Jennifer Jordan—Mt. Vernon, Texas
   Anise Shapiro—Plano, Texas

2. Pat Wright—Mt. Vernon, Texas

3. Mary Shaw—Little Rock, Arkansas

4. Lori Spears—Albuquerque, New Mexico

5. Jill Hargrove—Houston, Texas

6. Carol Kennedy—Longview, Texas

7. Barbara Reed—Norman, Oklahoma

8. Sue Baker—Oklahoma City, Oklahoma

9. Louise McKinney—Las Vegas, Nevada

10. Sarah Lee—Ft. Smith, Arkansas

TOP PRIVATE PILOTS (LESS THAN 200 HOURS)

1. Rick Shockey—Little Rock, Arkansas
   Henry Friesen—Paris, Texas
   Keith Penny—Sulphur Springs, Texas

2. Kyle McKeever—Valliant, Oklahoma
   Steve Stewart—DeQueen, Arkansas

3. Brent Bolin—Idabel, Oklahoma

4. TJ Crews—Rome, Georgia

5. Mark Kennemore—Ashdown, Arkansas

6. Darren Milner—Valliant, Oklahoma

7. Ray Ricketts—Broken Bow, Oklahoma

8. Brian Hunt—Winnsboro, Texas

9. Ronnie Foster—Winnsboro, Texas

10. Bill Thompson—Winnsboro, Texas

11. Russell Phillips—Idabel, Oklahoma

12. Chris Methvin—Hugo, Oklahoma

13. Jacob Friesen—Paris, Texas

14. David Webb—Atlanta, Texas

15. Peter Wieler—Sumner, Texas

16. Cody Lankford—Bonham, Texas

17. Mike Schewmaker—Texarkana, Texas
    Jacob Morris—Idabel, Oklahoma

TOP PILOTS (200-400 HOURS)

1. Seth Hayes—Idabel, Oklahoma
   Justin Bateman—Lindale, Texas
   Kent McClure—Atlanta, Texas
   Dane McGee—Greenville, Texas
   Kevin Edwards—Campbell, Texas

2. Michael Russell—Paris, Texas
   Tim Bowlin—Locksburg, Arkansas

3. Zach Taylor—Texarkana, Texas
   Glyn Thrash—Ashdown, Texas

4. AJ Waters—Atlanta, Texas

5. Brad Snider—Idabel, Oklahoma
   Brian Snider—Idabel, Oklahoma

6. Larry Hughes, Mineola, Texas

7. Craig Kizer—Mineola, Texas

8. Wayne Stafford—Clarksville, Texas

9. Tony Johnson—DeQueen, Arkansas

10. Duane Birdsong—Idabel, Oklahoma

11. Kevin Edwards—Campbell, Texas

12. Jacob Wieler—Petty, Texas

13. Dustin Hughes—Texarkana, Texas

14. AC Self—Campbell, Texas

15. Henry Dean—Texarkana, Arkansas

Top Instrument Pilots (300-1,000 Hours)

1. Shawn Francis—Hugo, Oklahoma
   Shawn Harmon—Idabel, Oklahoma
   Cody Stafford—Clarksville, Texas

2. Dr. Mark Campbell—Paris, Texas
   Dr. Mike Hutchins—Paris, Texas
   John Knight—DeQueen, Arkansas
   Gary Packnett—DeQueen, Arkansas

3. Howard Covington—DeQueen, Arkansas
   Dale Jordan—Mt. Vernon, Texas

4. Jessie Shipman—Honey Grove, Texas
   Ricky Hevron—Honey Grove, Texas

5. Jimmy Symers, Paris, Texas

6. John Hill—Longview, Texas

7. Wayne Smith—Longview, Texas

8. Dennis Walker—Tyler, Texas

9. Wylie Hockett—Petty, Texas

10. Dennis Seaburg—Las Vegas, Nevada

Top Commercial Pilots (Less than 600 Hours)

1. Shawn Harmon—Idabel, Oklahoma
   Steve Davis—Texarkana, Texas
   Steve Bell—Broken Bow, Oklahoma

2. Dean Smith—Broken Bow, Oklahoma
   Seth Hayes—Idabel, Oklahoma

3. Kent Walker—Idabel, Oklahoma

4. Larue Allen—Grand Saline, Texas

5. Chriss Hoss—Broken Bow, Oklahoma

6. Vernon Murphy—Texarkana, Texas

7. Gary Milner—Valliant, Oklahoma

8. Kent McClure—Atlanta, Texas

9. AJ Waters—Atlanta, Texas

10. Zach Taylor—Texarkana, Texas

TOP COMMERCIAL PILOTS (OVER 600 HOURS)

1. Ronnie Webb—Hobbs, New Mexico
   Tommy Hanks, Jr.—Mt. Vernon, Texas
   Weldon Garrison—Ashdown, Arkansas
   Cody Stafford—Clarksville, Texas
   Carl Standridge—Texarkana, Texas

2. Ricky Hevron—Honey Grove, Texas
   Jessie Shipman—Honey Grove, Texas
   Mike Stauter—Valliant, Oklahoma
   Bryan Stauter—Idabel, Oklahoma

3. Scott Simmons—DeQueen, Arkansas
   Joe Greer—DeQueen, Arkansas

4. Randy Bateman—Lindale, Texas

5. Dennis Walker—Tyler, Texas

6. Bob Gee—Tyler, Texas
   Kevin Gee—Mt. Vernon, Texas

7. Dwight Francis—Valliant, Oklahoma

8. Johnny Davis—Texarkana, Texas

9. Quinton Harris—Big Sandy, Texas

10. Rex Johnson—Tyler, Texas
    Randy Johnson—Tyler, Texas

SMALL COMPLEX PILOTS

1. Tommy Hanks—Mt. Vernon, Texas
   Shawn Francis—Hugo, Oklahoma
   Carl Standridge—Texarkana, Texas
   Grant Webb—Tulsa, Oklahoma
   Bobby Tucker—Broken Bow, Oklahoma

2. Ricky Hevron—Honey Grove, Texas
   Jessie Shipman—Honey Grove, Texas

3. Tony Burrow—Ashdown, Arkansas
   G.A. Merryworth—Lone Oak, Texas

4. Kerry Stepp—Athens, Texas
   Steve Davis—Texarkana, Texas

5. Bryan Hackney—Paris, Texas
   Garland Pool—Athens, Texas

6. Dean Smith—Broken Bow, Oklahoma

7. Larue Allen—Grand Saline, Texas

8. John Knight—DeQueen, Arkansas

9. Rex Johnson—Tyler, Texas

10. Randy Johnson—Tyler, Texas

LARGE COMPLEX TOP PILOTS

1. Tom Hanks—Leesburg, Texas
   Dr. Dan Bookout—Texarkana, Texas
   Jennifer Jordan—Mt. Vernon, Texas
   Anise Shapiro—Plano, Texas
   Gregg "Tex" Roberts—Winnsboro, Texas

2. Scott Simmons—DeQueen, Arkansas
   Dwight Francis—Valliant, Oklahoma

3. Mike Stauter—Valliant, Oklahoma
   Bryan Stauter—Valliant, Oklahoma

4. JR Richey—Paris, Texas
   Scott Jackson—Paris, Texas

5. Dale Jordan—Mt. Vernon, Texas
   Randy Bateman—Lindale, Texas

6. Dennis Walker—Tyler, Texas
   Scott Glover—Mt. Pleasant, Texas

7. Gene Moore—Mt. Pleasant, Texas
   John Golightly—Mt. Pleasant, Texas

8. QD Harris—Tyler, Texas

9. Kevin Gee—Mt. Vernon, Texas

10. Bob Gee—Tyler, Texas

My Dream of Becoming a Millionaire

I started working with kids when I was a kid myself. I was 16 years old growing up in Idabel, Oklahoma. I had 3 paper routes and needed other kids to help me. I usually hired boys that came from poor homes or broken families. These kids usually needed the basics: food, clothes, and transportation. I ended up spending more for their needs than I was earning from 3 paper routes.

I learned something about myself at that early age. I enjoyed helping and giving to others. Those things are still part of my character today.

At the age of 20, I started coaching little league baseball in the summer and coaching junior league basketball in the winter. I also directed a boys club in my early 20s. I agreed to direct a boys club for 2 years in Farmington, New Mexico. There is where I really learned to help a lot of kids and how much money it costs. I bought them clothes, shoes, food, and sometimes a little spending money. In short, I could not make enough money with a full time job and two or three part time jobs.

There were times I would delay my own house payment to help others. Then, I realized that was not fair to my own family, so I came up with an idea. If I became a millionaire, I would enjoy giving it to others and of course take care of my own family. I started working for an oil and gas company 4 days a week and started spending my 3 days off doing anything I could to earn money. Then, I learned that you cannot become a millionaire working for someone else.

This desire drove me to flying and teaching flying on the weekends. I was so desperate to earn my million dollars. I tried almost everything part time. I sold insurance, pots, and pans. I even sold vacuum cleaners and sewing machines on the Navajo Indian Reservation in New Mexico. I learned something else about myself. I wanted to earn a million dollars but not at the expense of others. For example, on Saturdays Allen, a Navajo Indian guide, had a radio show in Farmington, New Mexico. He spoke both English and Navajo. Then, he and I would go out on the reservation on Saturdays and sale house hold goods to the Navajos. They lived in Hogans. They had no electricity or running water. They had the biggest thing that we needed. They had a lot of money from oil and mineral rights. I remember one Saturday; we went out and sold a lot of vacuum cleaners and sewing machines. We were making large commissions on each item. I would split with Allen. That Saturday night while we were eating a late supper, I thought and then said to Allen, "I just realized something. We sold those people a lot of electrical appliances, and they don't even have electricity!" Allen replied, "Don't worry Bob; they will get electricity in a few years. Just think, they will have all of the appliances already." I told Allen that I was desperate to earn money but not at the expense of others. I want to help others. That was my last sale and last trip to the Indian reservation.

I read an ad in the Farmington Paper that said that pilots were needed to fly oil workers to different parts of the country. At the time I did not know that you had to have a commercial pilot certificate to fly for hire. I went to the Farmington Airport on a Friday to and told him I wanted to learn to fly and get me one of those jobs. The owner told me that there was a lot involved in becoming a commercial pilot. He said that you have to start out as a private pilot and that we needed to get started.

I soon realized that I could not earn a million dollars flying for someone else. There just is not enough time in a day or week or month to work for others and achieve my goal. While practicing my commercial pilot ratings, I did some training from a piper dealer in Albuquerque, New Mexico. The instructor I had at the time was Garth Greenlee. He was an ambitious person and never wasted any of his life just getting by. He too was working different part time jobs to earn more money. He invited me to an Amway meeting, which was just getting started around 1959 to 1960. Today they are very successful worldwide. I joined and tried to make it work part time. I just could not find a way to sell enough soap to earn a million dollars. In fact over the past 40 years, I have tried Amway 8 different times to make it work. The reason I kept trying is because I met several pilots who had become millionaires in the Amway business. For myself, I just have not been able to make it work.

Over the years, I was able to achieve my commercial pilots and instructors ratings part time. While living in Tuscan, Arizona, I was teaching flying in the mid 70s, I was approached by a person to do some charter flying on weekends. I flew to Las Vegas to Salt Lake City, Utah to Bakersfield, California. I would be flying a Cessna 210 with all the seats removed except the pilot's seat. I asked him what the cargo would be, and he said pet rocks. I said, "Pet Rocks? What? You are kidding!" He said, "No, pet rocks are sweeping the country. We need to get in on it while it is a fad." I said that I would do it since the pay was good. The pay was 100 dollars per hour with expenses. My biggest load in the beginning was to Las Vegas on Saturdays. I could haul up to a thousand pounds of pet rocks small, medium, and large all in separate little bags. At the time, we had 3 vendors in Las Vegas, and they would meet me at the North Las Vegas Airport to pick up the pet rocks. Then I would fly back to Tuscan and pick up an order for Salt Lake City, Utah.

The man who owned the pet rock business had a rock crushing plant just outside of Tuscan. I got to know him really well, and his nick name was "Rocky" of course. I told Rocky one day that if people are buying pet rocks, surely they would buy a bed for their pet rock to sleep in at night. Rocky said that was a good idea. He told me to patent a rock bed, so I did. I have the franchise for beds for pet rocks. Boy was I excited, I could just see it. I would sell them in each state. I would sell people their own franchise for beds for pet rocks. We had small, medium, and large rock beds made out of paper cartons and straw. I was going to be rich. Finally, I was going to be a millionaire. I added it up: 50 states with 20,000 per franchise. That comes to a million dollars. I could not wait, so I got started. Rocky would fabricate the beds at his Tuscan plant, and I would make the sale. I sold one of the vendors in Las Vegas 5,000 beds for pet rocks. The cost was $2.50 for small, $3.50 for medium, and $4.50 for large. They would add $1.50 for profit. I was excited because I was on my way to becoming a millionaire selling rock beds. Like most things that I have tried in my life, it was too little too late. I found out I was short of Rocky at the end of 2 years. He had already made his 2 million in the pet rock business and was ready to move back to California to buy a restaurant and motel in Bakersfield, California. His manager in Tuscan bought him out, mainly just to get the land where the rock company was located. His manager wanted to build homes on the land to sell.

The pet rock craze started fading. Rocky sold the 210 that I was flying and that ended my charter flying. It also ended my dream of becoming a millionaire selling rock beds. At the time I was a captain in the army reserve and had the opportunity to assume a 3 year command of a USAR unit in Las Vegas. I moved to Las Vegas in 1974 and taught flying on weekends. After my tour was up in Las Vegas, I moved to Tyler, Texas so that my son Kenny, who was 10 at the time, could grow up around family.

In Tyler, I got a sales job with Welex of Halliburton. I had a company car and expense account, which included 8 game tickets to the Dallas Cowboy football games. Our job was logging and perforating oil and gas wells in East Texas.

I have always enjoyed coaching and working with kids. I coached Babe Ruth Baseball. My son Kenny played on the team. I also coached him in football at the Mission Christian Academy in Tyler. Kenny was the quarterback, and I was the head coach. Now that was a challenge. All parents want their kid to play quarterback. I was fortunate that as a sophomore, Kenny was the fastest and the best player on the team at 5'5" and 135 pounds. One Friday night against the Lancaster Christian Academy of Dallas, Kenny ran and passed for 5 touchdowns, which earned him All East Texas player of the week. At the end of his sophomore year, he decided to give up football and pursue tennis and karate kick boxing. He obtained his black belt and won the Southwest Junior Championships in Dallas, Texas at the age of 16. While in high school, Kenny had 86 fights and won 82 of them. After high school Kenny joined the Marines for 6 years.

During this period of time, I still had the desire and dream of becoming a millionaire, so I could help others. I have had as many as 5 part time jobs t earn money. Anything from teaching night classes at Tyler and Kilgore Junior Colleges to selling Britannica encyclopedias to delivering pizzas to mowing yards. I also taught flying. You name it, and I have probably done it. People would ask me why at 60 years old did I work 5 jobs. I would just say that I wanted to make money.

I am publishing the book mainly to leave my family and friends something to remember me by not to earn a million dollars. Of course it would be nice to sell a few copies, but at this time in my life there is still hope of earning a million dollars. How? I think I will earn my million dollars in the Healthy Chocolate Business.

My two good friends and pilots that I trained appear in this book. Rick Shockley and Ronnie Webb are well on their way of becoming millionaires in just 3 years. We have been in the Healthy Chocolate Business together for the past 3 years. They are now full time flying all over the world holding seminars about the benefits of Healthy Chocolate. I, of course, am only part time so far. I am wanting to finish this book, which is now finished. The second addition will be out in September of 2009. Now that the book is finished, I can spend more time on my Healthy Chocolate Business. I am excited, and you can still get excited at the age of 73. My volume in the Healthy Chocolate Business has increased in the past 3 years to 949,000 volume. Your volume remains in storage as long as you order a small order each month. By the end of the year, because so many people are joining us in the Healthy Chocolate Business just part time, Jeanice and my volume will exceed a million dollars by the end of 2009. Our volume is listed under Terry Enterprises.

That does not necessarily mean that we will become millionaires, but we sure have the opportunity in the Healthy Chocolate Business.

Lord bless you and keep you! I will see you on the mountain tops! Thanks for sharing your time.

Bobby K. Terry Sr. CFII

Double Diamond MXICORP Healthy Chocolate

Email: *bkt@beloemail.com*

Phone: 903-782-9778
         903-286-3558

Tom Hanks
Leesburg, Texas
Private and Complex Pilot
Tom was the first student to every fly solo at the Mount Vernon, Texas Airport. CFII Bob
Terry cutting Tom's shirt tail.

Bobby K. Terry, SR. with wife Jeanice Terry (Paris, TX)

Clova and Kenny Terry. Tyler, Texas.

Elsie Barker "Mamaw Barker". Mother and Mother-in-law of Jeanice and Bob K. Terry Sr.
(Hagensport, TX)

Wanda Jo Jackson & husband Charles (Bob's sister and brother-in-law)
(Idabel, OK)

Private, Instrument, Commercial Pilot Jack Webb. Idabel, OK. (nephew of Bob K. Terry Sr.)

Jimmy Dan and Margaret Barker. Hagansport, TX. Brother and Sister in Law to Jeanice Terry.

Joe and Joy Barker. Hagansport, Texas. Brothers and Sister n law to Jeanice Terry.

Leona Sowell and Betty Buchannon

Private Pilot and FAA Medical Examiner Dr. Robert White & wife Pat (Mt. Vernon, TX)

Minister Patrick Cannon and wife Kari Ann. Paris, Texas.

Minister Jim Parker and wife Shirley. Mt. Pleasant, Texas.

Minister John & Martha Mullins (Hagensport, TX)

Minister Neal Thurman and family. Tracy, Andy, and Spencer Thurman. Tyler, Texas.

Minister Keith Penny. Sulphur Springs, Texas. Peerless Christian Academy. Private Pilot.

Index of Photos (Listed in order of response)

Jodi—Valliant, OK

102   Teresa, Jodi, Cheryl
       Rick

103   Robert Watson—Shreveport, LA
       Shawn and Chandler Francis—Hugo, OK

104   Jerry L. Robinson—Hot Springs, AR
       Dr. Dan and Phyllis Bookout—Texarkana, TX

105   Eddie G. Hill—Atlanta, TX
       Phyllis Bookout—Texarkana, TX

106   Brandi Richey—Pattonville, TX
       Tommy Hanks—Pittsburg, TX

107   Robert Starnes—Weesbaben, Germany
       Aniso Shapiro—Plano, Tax

108   Wesley Bates—Antlers, OK
       Michael Hutchins—Paris, TX

109   Ray Ricketts—Broken Bow, OK
       Chris Sibley—Commerce, TX

110   Skyler Burchinal—Paris, TX
       Glen Chapman—Paris, TX

111   Christy Taylor and Hunter Bramlett—Paris, TX
       Bryan Hackney—Paris, TX

112   Chet Glenn—Hugo, OK
       Darrell Frost—Atlanta, TX

113   Todd Chiles—Dallas, TX
       Charles and Lisa Avila—Bonham, TX

114   Brittany Miller—Blossom, TX
       Beau Chapman—Blossom, TX

115   George Whelton—Idabel, OK
       Kent McClure—Atlanta, TX

116   Tony Burrow—Ashdown, AR
       Gregg Roberts—Winnsboro, TX

117   Peter Wieler—Petty, TX

118   Jacob Wieler—Petty, TX

119   Johnny Davis—Texarkana, TX
       Steven A. Davis—Texarkana, TX

120   Weldon and Jace Garrison—Ashdown, AR
       David Gillete—Mt. Pleasant, TX

121   Regg (Will) Wilsford—Bonham, TX
       Randall Low—Antlers, OK

122   Eric You—Lone Oak, TX
       Ray Burch—Van, TX

123   Sydney B. Hale Jr. and Mary Gail Hale—Bonham, TX

Courtney Hevron and nephews—Honey Grove, TX

124   Wayne Stafford—Clarksville, TX
Cody Stafford—Clarksville, TX

125   Brian and Amy Snider—Idabel, OK
Dean and Connie Smith—Broken Bow, OK

126   Rebekah Smith and Jason Hayes and child—Broken Bow, OK
Dean and Connie Smith and Rebekah Smith and Jason Hayes—Broken Bow, OK

127   Sheila Anders—Mt. Vernon, TX
Kaleb Dyer—Mt. Vernon, TX

128   Debbie Keith—Mt. Vernon, TX
Barbara Todd—Lone Oak, TX

129   Kristin and Konnor Burgin—Lone Oak, TX
Josie House—Mt. Pleasant. Barbara Todd—Lone Oak, TX

130   Alan Phillips—Broken Bow, OK
Chris Methvin and family—Hugo, OK

131   Harold Stone—Winnsbor, TX
Kyle McKeever and family—Hugo, OK

132   Alan Phillips and family—Broken Bow, OK
Dexter Tan—Long Beach, CA

207   Snider family—Idabel, OK

207   Brad Snider and family—Idabel, OK
Brad Snider—Idabel, OK

210   James Napurano and Adam Koropsak—Addison, TX
Jim Folks—Greenville, TX

211   Sean Vaughn—Arkadelphia, AR
Jenny Wei

212   Adam Kordsmeier—Conway, AR
Nathan Gerth—Arkadelphia, AR

213   Jason Minchew—Arkadelphia, AR
Brian Grizzle—Arkadelphia, AR

214   Nathan Bradshaw
Brandon Herring

215   Forrest Martin—Arkadelphia, AR
Clay Phillips

216   Andrew Williams—Clernedon, AR
Corey Hatfield—Cedarville, AR

217   Troy Hogue—Arkadelphia, AR
Robert Stephenson—Arkadelphia, AR

218   Bart Hausen—Santa Ava, CA
       Conrad McEachern—Dallas, TX
219   Winn Harris—Lewisville, TX
       Ben Mangan—Davenport, IA
220   James Finley—Greenville, TX
       Ted Myers—Greenville, TX
221   Nick Russman—Merit, TX
       Lyndol Erwin—Greenville, TX
222   Peter Zaccagnino—Flemington, NJ
       Mark Hanson—Locust Grove—GA
223   Michael Luce—Greenville, TX
       Steven and Ina Schmillen—Elkhorn, NE. Alyda and Phil Ladenthin—
       Elkhorn, NE
224   Jeff Jennings—Oklahoma City, OK. Robert Terry—Yukon, OK
225   Bob DeMunck—Allen, TX
       Kevin Groves—Allen, TX
226   Larry Hughes and Julie Vaughn—Allen, TX
227   Boyd L. Wheeler—Shreveport, LA
       Tim Mers—Haughton, LA
228   Dr. Mark Campbell—Paris, TX
       Jason Mars—Mt. Pleasant, TX
229   Rance Campbell—Mt. Pleasant, TX
       Philip Greenspan—Cambridge, MA
230   Norman Haase—Ft. Townson, OK
       David Gillette, Rance Campbell, Jason Mars—Mt. Pleasant, TX
231   Rachael Meziere—Lavon, TX
       Jim, Dianne, and Melody Carr—Winnsboro, TX
232   Ricky King—Winnsboro, TX
       Bob and Maega Snow—Rattan, OK
233   Ronnie and Amy Foster—Winnsboro, TX
       Robert and Harley Franklin—Greenville, TX
234   Jerry and Brandi Richey—Pattonville, TX
       Heath Roberts—Winsboro, TX
235   Ray Elgin—Winnsboro, TX
       Darren Coach—Celina, TX
236   Carl Elkins—Winnsboro, TX
       Buzz Payne and Mike Sheeley—Big Sandy, TX

237   Jessie Shipman—Honey Grove, TX
Jack Ashmore—Paris, TX
249   TJ Crews—Rome, GA
Mark and Kinder Kennemore—Ashdown, AR
238   Jacob and Jealene Friesen—Paris, TX
Pete Buhler—Paris, TX
239   Gregg "Tex" and Shae Roberts—Winnsboro, TX
Shae Roberts—Winnsboro, TX
240   Robert Suddeth—Mineola, TX
Al and Nancy Shuele—Austin, TX
241   Don Willingham—Brashear, TX
Rex Heminger and Kris Elkund—Dallas, TX
242   Tim and Kim Knox—Paris, TX
Joe Kochick and Lindsey Oldham—Paris, TX
243   Larry Smith—Pagusa Springs, CO
Patrick Jenevein—Dallas, TX
244   Mark Parsons and Dick Stephens—Richardson, TX
Sam Massey—Paris, TX
245   Zach Reeder—Mojave, CA
Gerald Carmack—Jasper, TX
246   David Herbert, Mike Jenike, Kevin Herbert—San Angelo, TX
William Brizzon—Greenville, TX
247   Chad D. Parrott—Paris, TX
Bill Booth—Paris, TX
248   C. Olmsted and Morgan Joslin—Sulphur Springs, TX
Cody Stephens and Jimmy Smyers—Paris, TX
249   Martin Meyer—Albuquerque, New Mexico
TJ and Jim Crews—Idabel, OK
250   Rusty McClahan, Marin Tomulet, Steve Lopez—Dallas, TX
Marin Tomulet
251   Steve Dean—Gilmer, TX
Michael G. Coco—Paris, TX
252   Donnie Royal—Quinlan, TX
Ed Mason and Cliff Gerber—Westlinn, OR
253   Peter Fox—Tyler, TX
Steve Schauer—3-Rivers, MI

254	Vinnie Grando—Boerne, TX
	Richad Freeman—Denton, TX
255	Brandon Powell—Athens, TX
	Darrell Wright—Big Sandy, TX
256	Ray Burch—Grand Saline, TX
	Troy Robinson—Quitman, TX
257	Larry Lowe—Seminole, OK
	Kent Walker—Idabel, OK
258	Jim Martin Sr.—Marietta, TX
	Jim Martin Jr.—Naples, TX
259	Jim and Annette Martin Sr.—Marietta, TX
	Jim Martin Sr. and Jr.
260	Aubrie Turner—Atlanta, TX
	Aubrie Turner
261	Robert R. Hicks—Idabel, OK
	Brent Bolen—Idabel, OK
262	Ruth Ann King—Bonham, TX
	Bubba Coston—Paris, TX
263	Charles W. Davis—Paris, TX
	Philip Whitaker—Paris, TX
264	Wilbur and Wilson Cox—Texarkana, TX
	Walter DeVore—Texarkana, TX
265	Ray Hull—Waynoka, OK
	Wesley Rawle and Marlianna Sander—Emory, TX
266	Brian Hunt—Winnsboro, TXS
	Brian Hunt and family—Winnsboro, TX
267	R. L. Ratliff and Roy Truitt—Addison, TX
	Vernon Murphy and Pooh Wade—Texarkana, TX
268	Dennis Mathis—Greenville, TX
	Gary Gallandat and Bill Talutis—Echo Lake, TX
269	Cody Roberts—Winnsboro, TX
	Gregg Roberts—Winnsboro, TX
270	Dean Smith—Broken Bow, OK
	Nathan Smith—Broken Bow, OK
271	David Yturri—Dallas, TX
	Tom Travis—Dallas, TX
272	James and Margaret Ashmore—Bonham, TX
	Noland Ashmore and family—Bonham, TX
272	Norman Moorehead—Bivins, TX
	Steven A. and Carolyn Davis—Texarkana, TX
318	Jacob, Courtney, and Jennifer—Idabel, OK
	Jacob Morris—Idabel, OK

274	Charles and Carl Johnson—Barksdale AFB, LA
	Michael O. Feavel—Benton, LA
275	James Walker—Shreveport, LA
	Gayle L. Robinson Jr.—Marshall, TX
276	Joe Provenza—Bossier City, LA
	Richard Krouskop—Bellingham, WA
277	Brad Schmidt—Shreveport, LA
	Walter L. Cook Sr.—Bossier City, LA
278	Jimmy Smyers—Paris, TX
	Richard Yazell—Gilmer, TX
279	Chris Hoss—Broken Bow, OK
	Jim Henderson—Greenville, TX
280	LaRue Allen—Lindale, TX
	Paul Lindsey—Quinlan, TX
315	Glyn Thrash—Ashdown, AR
	Harry Andonian—Greenville, TX
281	Boyd Proctor—Leesburg, TX
	Brian Proctor—Porterville, CA
282	Kevin Herrington—Honey Groe, TX
	Jason Redubs—Paris, TX
283	Tom Noble—Winnsboro, TX
	AJ, Dana, and Haylee Waters—Atlanta, TX
284	Tevis Pappas—Atlanta, TX
	Paul C. Smeltzer—Texarkana, TX
295	Zack Taylor—Texarkana, TX
	Lorenzo and Laurence Lasater—Greenville, TX
285	Joe and Debbie Erbs—Enid, OK
	Gene and Karen Pearcey—Durango, CO
286	Josh Jorgenson—Arkadelphia, AR
	Joe Don Burlsworth—Harrison, AR
287	Paul Turnlison—Montecelo, AR
	John Knight—DeQueen, AR
288	LaRue Allen—Grand Saline, TX
	Tim Parson Jr.—Benton, AR
289	Nick Boyd—Arkadelphia, AR
	Jonathan Moss—Atlanta, TX
290	Richard Yazell, Sheadon Williams, and Tommy Moore
	Jesse and Allison Loftin
291	Jonathan Self—Campbell, TX
	A.L. Self—Campbell, TX
292	A.L. and Kathy Self—Campbell, TX
	Jonathan Self and family—Campbell, TX

295 Zach Taylor—Texarkana, TX
   Noah Rogers—Maud, TX
293 Jim Crews—Millerton, Ok
   Roy and Betty Peevy—Broken Bow, OK
294 Gary L. Rickey—Foreman, AR
   Becky Wilemon—Shreveport, LA
133 Henry Dean—Texarkana, TX. Benny Blaylock—Norman, OK
   Seth and Terry Hayes—Idabel, OK
134 Eddie Hill and Paula—Hughes Springs, TX
   Loren Bond—Atlanta, TX
135 William Thompson—Winnsboro, TX
   Kevin and Brandon Edwards—Campbell, TX
136 Stan Stamper and Mike Ahern
137 Perney Taylor Webb, Bill Webb, and Francis Webb
   Paul—Oklahoma City, OK
138 Misty Mitchell and Eugene Smith—Antlers, OK
   Clinton Lewis—Antlers, OK
139 Wilma Avery and Bill Middleton—Hugo, OK
   JN and Sharon Rhodes—Hugo, OK
140 Carolyn Moseley, Andrea Wright, Bailey, Colton, Josie, and Stormie—
   Hugo, OK
   Zach and Kalan Maxwell—Hugo, OK
141 Shawn and Chandler Francis—Hugo, OK
   Charles and Sue Cousin—Hugo, OK
142 Wanda Ward—Hugo, OK
   Dorsey and Dee Myers—Hugo, OK
143 Denise Hill—Oklahoma City, OK
   Chet Glenn and Joe Bunn—Hugo, OK
144 Donna Abbott—Hugo, OK
   Gladys Sharp, Carla Rhodes, and Samuel Rhodes—Hugo and Sawyer,
   OK
145 Ray and Ann Jordan—Hugo, OK
   Sheila Beard, Karla Cope, Jody Rawis, Kalyn, and Tristen—Hugo, OK
   and Paris, TX
146 Lawan Wood—Hugo, OK
   Christina Capers, Angela Sparks, Debbie Park, Roy Lyles, Alyssa Wright,
   Ethan Sparks
147 Joe Webb—Hugo, OK
   Penny Harvey, Tom Nation, and Kacy Barlo—California and Soper, OK
148 Amy Morris—Ft. Worth, TX
   Kay Fox, Nancy Wise, Howard Wise, and Ruth Josey—Rockwall, TX,
   Arlington, TX, and Oklahoma City, OK

149   Danny Johnson—Plano, TX
        Eddie and Chelsi Glenn—Hugo, OK

150   Antonio Turner—Texarkana, TX
        David and Donna Webb—Atlanta, TX

151   Robert Jacobs—Denton, TX
        Brian Davis—Durant, OK

152   Jordan Powell—Wylie, TX
        Andrew Lilley

153   Brittan Kirk—Oklahoma City, OK
        Brenton Porter—Gainesville, TX

154   Chris Glenn—Durant, OK
        Zachary Smith—Durant, OK

155   Travis Smith—Greenville, TX
        Blayze Perkins—Grapevine, TX

156   Anthony Johnson—DeQueen, AR
        KT Grantham—Dallas, TX

157   Tyler Dunn—Melissa, TX
        Austin McCann—Foothill Ranch, CA

158   Cole Cissell—Durant, OK
        Jon Cobb—Lelina, TX

159   Steven Kester—Sarasota, FL
        Chris Barthel—Oklahoma City, OK

160   Paul Schad—Gainesville, TX
        Steve Libick—Denotn, TX

161   George Jacox—Durant, OK
        Ben Kenagg—Cedar Park, TX

162   Walt—Idabel, OK
        Teresa—Idabel, OK

163   Cheryl—Idabel, OK
        Teresa—Idabel, OK

164   Vicki—Commerce, TX
        Jeff—Mineola, TX

165   Daryl—Broken Bow, OK
        Jerry—Broken Bow, OK

166   Susan and Jeff
        Darrell—Idabel, OK

167   Daryl—Broken Bow, OK
        Cheryl—Idabel, OK

168   Allen—Idabel, OK
        Sue and Ronnie—Idabel, OK

169   Jake—Bochito, OK
        Jones—Lindale, TX

170	Mickey—Idabel, OK
	David—Idabel, OK
171	Norman—Idabel, OK
	Jack—Idabel, OK
172	Joe—Gilmer, TX
	Mark—Mt. Pleasant, TX
173	Max McLeod
	Wes McMillon—DeKalb, TX
174	Bill Murdock Jr.—Texarkana, TX
	Carl Staudridge Jr.—Texarkana
175	Mike Shewmaker—Texarkana
	Rachael Shewmaker—Texarkana
176	Jim Martin Jr.—Marietta, TX
	Larry Weaver—Atlanta, TX
177	Paul Tanner—Bonham, TX
	Dr. Gusky—Gilmer, TX
178	Austin Cude—Tulsa, OK
	Klass and Celistino Banman—Petty, TX
179	Justin Lee—Maud, TX
	J.K. Weger—Paris, TX
180	Peter Harder Zacharias—Tigertown, TX
	Peter Zacharias and Henry Friesen—Tigertown, TX and Paris, TX
181	Josh Cantrell—Jacksonville, AR
	Joe Bunn—Hugo, OK
182	Bill Allan—Sulphur Springs, TX
	Jesse Shipman—Honey Grove, TX
183	Cris Bookout—Texarkana, TX
	Richard Gumber—Texarkana, TX
184	David W. Brown—Oklahoma City, OK
	Bob Newell—Yukon, OK
185	Scott Hurley—Emory, TX
	Dennis Harwell—Telephone, TX
186	Phil Hale—Nacogdoches, TX
	John E. Hines—Points, TX
187	Kenneth Taylor—Bonham, TX
	Lou Peacock—Farmersville, TX
188	Matt Steward—Cumby, TX
	Walter Hixson—Magnolia, AR
189	Jake Harrell—Little Rock, AR
	Hunter Byram—Searcy, AR
190	Trey McCully—Wylie, TX
	Peter Wieler—Paris, TX

191	Wesley Bates. Emma, Donna, and Ronnie Branton—Antlers, OK
	Jace Garrison—Ashdown, AR
192	Rick and Rikki Shockley—Little Rock, AR
193	Ronnie Webb—Hobbs, New Mexico
194	Steve Stewart—DeQueen, AR
	Grant Smith—DeQueen, AR
195	Trevor Childs—DeQueen, AR
	Trevor Childs with Son Gabriel
196	Bill High—Hot Springs, AR
	Joe Greer—DeQueen, AR
197	Kent McClure—Atlanta, TX
	Dr. Mark Campbell with son Josh—Paris, TX
198	Chris Hill—Idabel, OK
	Robert Timmer—Broken Bow, OK
199	M. T. Schario—Marble Falls, TX
	Tom Shivey—Greenville, TX
200	Bob F. Young—Mineola, TX
	Randy Garrison and Larry Ford—Queen City, TX
201	Roger Parks—Dallas, TX
	Mike Anderson—Muskogee, OK
202	John Boyd—Little Rock, AR
	Major Wil Vessey, USMC with wife Corie—Corpus Christi, TX
203	Jim and James Campbell—Idabel, OK
204	Duanne Birdsong with wife Sharon—Idabel, OK
	Shawn Francis with son Chandler—Hugo, OK
205	Chelsea Peacock—Honey Grove, TX
	G.A. Merryworth—Lone Oak, TX
206	Buck Hill with wife Natalie—Idabel, OK

Jared Hicks – Hooper born August 22, 1984, and passed on May 14, 2003. He lived in Pittsburg, Texas, the first 4 years of his life and Mt. Vernon, Texas the rest. He attended Mt. Vernon Schools K-12th Grade. He was an active member of First Baptist Youth Group and a member of the school band, he loved playing guitar. In school he was involved in UIL Math and Computer Science teams, also member of Who's Who among American High School Students and the National Honor Society. Jared had one sister, Cecily Hooper. Jared was interested in planes and flying from a very young age. After he became a teenager, he thought he might want to fly fighter jets in the Armed Forces. About the age of 14, he started asking to take flying lessons a friend of ours. Tom Hanks told us about Bob Terry, flight instructor and so we paid for a few lessons for a Christmas present. He absolutely loved flying!---Dayna Hooper

IN LOVING MEMORY AND THE DEDICATION OF THIS BOOK TO STUDENT PILOT JARED HICKS-HOOPER

I met Jared in January of 1999. His folks had given him a 10 hour dual flying gift certificate as a Christmas gift. We started with a C-150 (Cessna) trainer at the Mt. Vernon, Texas airport. I was amazed how fast Jared learned all phases of flight instructions. S-turns, turn around a point, 360 degrees steep turns, slow flight power on power off stalls, even spins. In fact after 2 0r 3 hours of training, Jared would asked me if could do stalls, steep turns and spins every lesson! Jared really enjoyed all phases of flying, he said he would like to continue flying to become a commercial pilot. We kept flying from time to time looking forward to his 16th birthday so he could solo. He became ill with Rhabdomyosalgrama, a form of cancer. Therefore he could not pass a 3rd class physical. Jared was such a joy and pleasure to be around as a teenager. He was one of the best teenage student pilots that I have ever flown with. There is no doubt in my mind that he could have become an outstanding commercial pilot. His parents, Dayna and Wesley Hooper, and I were so disappointed that Jared could not live his dream of aviation. We miss him very much. But we know he has his own pair of wings now.-------Bobby K. Terry, Sr. CFII

Bobby K. Terry Sr. CFII with Bobby K. Terry Jr. Student Pilot
(1988)

Barbara Todd (Lone Oak, TX). Debbie Keith (Mt. Vernon, TX). Daughters.

Debbie & Kenny Keith. Mt. Vernon, TX
(daughter and son-in-law of Bob K. Terry, SR and Jeanice)
To Kenny: You are missed and will always be remembered!
Deceased during the final stages of this book.

Stephen and Kristin Burgin (Lone Oak, TX). Grandchildren

Don Boulton (Idabel, OK). FAA Written Test Proctor.
High School Football Teammate of Bobby K. Terry Sr.

Dick Logan (Idabel, OK). Church minister with wife Gloria.
High School Football Teammate of Bobby K. Terry Sr.

Gina Nelms. Gilmer, Texas. Private – Instrument. Debbie Baldwin. Mount Vernon, Texas. Private Pilot. Bobby Terry, Paris, Texas. CFII.

Jennifer Jordan, Mount Vernon, Texas. Commercial Pilot.

Betty Lou Jordan. Mother of Jennifer Jordan

Rick Shockley with his daughter Rikki Shockley
Little Rock, Arkansas
Private – Instrument Pilot
Double Diamond Executive (MXICORP) Healthy Chocolate
Rick enjoys traveling all over U.S. sharing his dream of success
in the Healthy Chocolate

Business with others. He saves time by flying himself privately.

Ronnie Webb
Hobbs, New Mexico
Private – Instrument – Commercial Pilot
Presidential Executive (MXICORP) Healthy Chocolate
Double Diamond

Ronnie and Naomi Webb

Ronnie and Naomi with their children and grandchildren

Pastor Dean Smith and wife Connie. Broken Bow, OK. Commercial Pilot. 1st Place Spot Landing Contest in Atlanta, TX.

Seth Hayes – Private Commercial Pilot. Seth is the son of Terry Hayes of Idabel, OK and Scott Hayes of Broken Bow, OK.

Seth is one of the most gifted student teenage pilots that I have ever flown with in 40 years of flight instruction. I only had to demonstrate one landing, and he took it from then o n. it's amazing! After teaching and coaching teenagers for over 40 years, Seth is one of the most polite and considerate young men that I have ever been associated with. After spending time with the rest of his family, I understand why he is so polite and considerate. Starting with his Aunt Shirley (one of the top female pilots in the country) and his cousin Shawn Harmond (the best of the best commercial pilot), everyone in his family flies. They have encouraged Seth to follow his dream in aviation. Seth is currently enrolled at Southeastern State College in Durant, OK. He is majoring in none other than aviation.

Seth Hayes with his mother Terry Hayes

Seth Hayes with Papa and Maw, Lewis & Marilyn James

Seth Hayes with his brother, Ian Hayes

Private Pilot Shirley Z. Smith, Seth's Aunt Idabel, OK

Commercial & Private Pilot Seth Hayes
Idabel, OK
My Aunt encouraged me to fly

Seth Hayes with Instructor Bob Terry

Kay McClure (Atlanta, TX). Female Pilot.

Private, Instrument, Commercial, & CFII Pilot Shawn Harmon with his family,
Le'erin, Tanna, Hayzn, and Laykn
Idabel, OK
To get to my hunting and fishing trips sooner!

Student Pilot Deborah Cole with children, River and Shanie
Paris, TX

Private, Instrument, and Commercial Pilot Dean Smith and Connie Smith
Broken Bow, OK
Started flying to finish a "God Call", into the mission field. I will continue to fly next to eaven waiting and anticipating Jesus to come in the air!

Student Pilot Jason Hayes
Broken Bow, OK
I enjoy being off the ground, it is a very good get away.
I get a peaceful feeling while flying.
Rebekah Smith, Nathan Smith, Heather Hayes

Commercial, Instrument, Multi-engine Pilot Scott Jackson
Paris, TX
Lifelong dream

Commercial, Instruction, Multi-engine Pilot Dwight Francis
Valliant, OK
Been flying for 50 years

1st Solo Flight-Shawn (Valliant, Oklahoma)

1st Solo Flight – Jodi (Valliant, Oklahoma)

1st Place – Teresa, Grand Champion – Jodi,
2nd Place – Cheryl Idabel, Oklahoma – July 1989

Grand Champion Male Pilot Division – Rick. Idabel, Oklahoma.

Private Pilot Robert Watson
Shreveport, LA

Private, Instrument, Commercial, & Multi-engine
Pilot Shawn Francis with Chandler Francis
Hugo, OK

ATP, ASEL, AMEL, ASES, C500, C650, Commercial Private Rotercraft Gyroplane,
CFI,CFII, CFIME, CFI R/W Helicopter, Designated Examiner, ASELM AMEL, Private and
Commercial, Instrument A & P Pilot Jerry L. Robinson
Hot Springs, AR

Private Instrument Commercial Single and Multi Engine ATP, Land and Sea CFI, CFII,
GROUND INSTRUCTOR Pilot Dr. Dan Bookout.
Flown around the world twice in single engine airplane holding 180 world records.
Shown with Grand Champion Spot Landing Contest winner wife, Phyllis Bookout.
Texarkana, TX

Private Pilot Eddie G. Hill
Atlanta, TX
Spot Landing Contest 1st Runner Up Adult Student Division Sept. 15, 2007
In Atlanta, TX

Sport Pilot Phyllis Bookout
Atlanta Spot Landing Contest 1st Runner Up Female Division
To keep up with my husband Dan!

Brandi Richey- Pattonville, TX

Tommy Hanks- Pittsburg, TX

A & P, Student Pilot Robert Starnes
Weesbaben, Germany
Everyone in my family files and now it's my turn

CFI/11, Multi-Engine, Lear Jet Type Pilot Anise Shapiro
Plano, TX
Love the beautiful skies, enjoyed the freedom, and having control of the airplane

Wesley Bates (Antlers, OK). He is a student pilot. He had first flying lesson on his 16th birthday

Michael Hutchins (Paris, TX) Private Pilot. Learning t fly has been his lifelong dream.

Sport Private Pilot Ray Ricketts
Broken Bow, OK
I began flying lessons in the 1970's because I simply enjoy being in the air and the freedom from ground restraints. I came close to getting my license, but due to circumstances beyond my control had to take a 35 year hirtus. Now I'm finishing what I started. It's a dream come true.

Student Pilot Chris Sibley
Commerce, TX
A thrill to be in the air!

Skyler Burchinal- Paris, TX

Glen Chapman (Paris, TX). Private Pilot

Student Pilots Christy Taylor & Hunter Bramlett
Paris, TX

Private, Instrument, commercial, Multi-Engine Pilot Bryan Hackney
Paris, TX
To maybe one day fly the heavy metal

Private, A&P, HLC Pilot Chet Glenn
Hugo, OK

Private & Instrument Pilot Darrell Frost
Atlanta, TX

Todd Chiles- Dallas, TX

Charles and Lisa Avila- Bonham, TX
Lisa – Private Pilot.
Paul Tanner (Bonham, TX). Private Pilot.

Student Pilot Brittany Miller
Blossom, TX
Lifelong Dream!

Student Pilot Beau Chapman
Blossom, TX
Ever since I was a little Boy I dreamed of flying!

ATP, 4-Type Ratings ASMEL, CFII, 46 years Commercial Pilot George Whelton
Idabel, OK
Great interest in airplanes love to fly, 1st flight 1950

Private, Instrument, Commercial, Multi-Engine Pilot Kent McClure
Atlanta, TX
Grand Champion Private Pilot Division 200-300 hours
Atlanta Spot Landing Contest Sept. 15, 2007
I want be a Commercial Pilot!

Private Instrument Commercial Pilot Tony Burrow
Ashdown, AR
Great way to travel (in business while taking my mind off the business)!

Private Instrument Commercial Multi-Engine CFI Pilot Gregg Roberts
Grand Champion Commercial Division over 1000 hours
Winnsborro, TX

Private Pilot Peter Wieler
Petty, TX
A hobby to get out and have fun.

Private Pilot Peter Wieler

Petty, TX

Private Instrument Cmmercial Pilot Jacob Wieler
Petty, TX
For a challenge!

Private Instrument commercial Pilot Jacob Wieler
Petty, TX

Private Instrument Commercial Pilot Johnny Davis
1st Runner Up Commercial Division over 600 Hours
Texarkana, AR

Private Instrument Commercial Pilot Steven A. Davis
Grand Champion Commercial Division over 400 hours
Texarkana, TX
My brother (pictured above) learned to fly and I wanted to prove to my Dad that I could too.

Weldon and Jace Garrison (Ashdown, AR). Commercial Pilot. Weldon congratulates his son Jace for receiving his Private Pilot License.

David Gilette (Mt. Pleasant, TX).
Private – Instrument Commercial Multi-Engine Pilot.
Lifelong dream to be a commercial pilot.

Private, Instrument, & commercial Pilot Regg (Will) Wilsford
Bonham, TX
It's a dream I've always had. My plane is named after my granddaughter J'cie Bella

Private & Instrument Pilot Randall Low
Antlers, OK
Mental Workout

737 Pilot Eric You
Lone Oak, TX
The Challenge!

Commercial, A&P, Radio Technician Ray Burch
Van, TX

A&P, Mechanic, & IA Pilot Sydney B. Hale, Jr.
Student Pilot Mary Gail Hale
Bonham, TX

Private Pilot Courtney Jones Hevron with nephews Trevor & Devin
Honey Grove, TX
Something I always wanted to do.

Private Pilot Wayne Stafford
Clarksville, TX
Got to be somewhere might as well be up in the air flying!

Private, Instrument, Commercial, CFII Pilot Cody Stafford
Clarksville, TX
To become a CFII and Commercial Pilot.

Private Pilot Brian Snider with wife Amy
Idabel, OK

Commercial Pilot Dean Smith with wife student Pilot Connie Smith
Broken Bow, OK
Pilot Dean Smith-Grand Champion Commercial Division Less 300 hours
Pilot Connie Smith 1st Runner Up Female Student Pilot Division
Atlanta Spot Landing Contest September 15, 2007

Student Pilot Rebekah Smith with fiancée Student Pilot Jason Hayes and Children Heather
Hayes and Nathan Smith
Broken Bow, OK
2nd Runner Up Female Student Pilot Division and 3rd Runner Up Student Pilot Division

Commercial Pilot Dean Smith with wife Student Pilot Connie Smith
And Daughter Student Pilot with her Fiancée Jason Hayes
Broken Bow, OK

Student Pilot Sheila Anders
Mt. Vernon, TX
Grand Champion Female Student Teenage Pilot Division
Atlanta, TX Spot Landing Contest, September 15, 2007

Student Pilot Kaleb Dyer
Mt. Vernon, TX
1st Runner Up Teenage Student Pilot Division
Atlanta, TX Spot Landing Contest, September 15, 2007

Student Pilot Debbie Keith
Mt. Vernon, TX
1st Runner Up Female Student Pilot Division
Atlanta, TX Spot Landing Contest, September 15, 2007

Student Pilot Barbara Todd
Lone Oak, TX
2nd Runner Up Female Student Pilot Division
Atlanta, TX Spot Landing Contest, September 15, 2007

Student Pilot Kristin Burgin with daughter Konnor Burgin (future pilot)
Lone Oak, TX
3rd Runner Up Female Student Pilot Division
Atlanta, TX Spot Landing Contest, September 15, 2007

Student Pilot Josie House with friend student pilot Barbara Todd
Mt. Pleasant, TX
4th Runner Up Female Student Pilot Division
Atlanta, TX Landing Contest, September 15, 2007

Private Pilot Chris Methvin
Broken Bow, OK
A Lifelong Dream!

Private Pilot Chris Methvin
Pictured with David Carlile, Cheyenne Methvin, Donna Methvin,
And Trevor Methvin all of Hugo, OK
I hate driving a vehicle and get out of the house!

Private Pilot Harold Stone
Winnsboro, TX
The thrill of going beyond the normal!

Private Pilot Kyle McKeever & Family
Valliant, OK
I have a dream of becoming a Commercial Pilot!

Private Instrument Commercial Pilot Alan Russell Phillips
Pictured with wife Rebecca and daughter Bethany
Broken Bow, OK

Instrument Commercial CFI/CFII Pilot Dexter Tan
LB, CA
Laid off from traveling job and wanted to continue traveling.

Private Pilot Henry Dean – Flight Examiner Mr. Benny Blaylock
Texarkana, AR – Norman, OK
Excitement of soaring with the eagles!

Private, Instrument, Commercial pilot Seth Hayes – Mother Terry Hayes
Idabel, OK
Dream of becoming a commercial pilot.

Private student Pilot Eddie Hill and friend Paula
1st Runner Up Adult Student Private Pilot
Hughes Springs, TX
I build airplanes and thought I might want to fly one.

Private Instrument Commercial Pilot Loren Bond
Atlanta, TX
I buy and sell airplanes!

Private Pilot William Thompson
Winnsboro, TX

Private Instrument Commercial Pilot Kevin Edwards with son Brandon Campbell, TX

Pilots Stan Stamper and Mike Ahern – Pilots of this N – 34
Hugo OK Air Show – October 2007

Families looking around at the air show
Hugo, OK air Show – October 2007

Perney Taylor Webb, Bill Webb and Francis Webb
Hugo OK Air Show – October 2007

Paul
Oklahoma City, OK
Hugo, OK Air Show – October 2007

Misty Mitchell and Eugene Smith
Antlers, OK
Hugo OK Air Show – October 2007

Clinton Lewis
Antlers, Ok
Hugo, OK Air Show – October 2007

Wilma Avery and Bill Middleton
Hugo, OK
Hugo OK Air Show – October 2007

JN and Sharon Rhodes
Hugo OK
Hugo, OK Air Show – October 2007

Carolyn Moseley, Andrea Wright, Bailey, Colton, Josie, and Stormie
Hugo, OK
Hugo OK Air Show – October 2007

Zach and Kalan Maxwell
Hugo OK
Hugo, OK Air Show - 2007

Shawn and Chandler Francis
Hugo, OK
Hugo OK Air Show - October 2007

Charles and Sue Cousin
Hugo OK
Hugo, OK Air Show – October 2007

Wanda Ward
Hugo, OK
Hugo OK Air Show – October 2007

Dorsey and Dee Myers
Hugo OK
Hugo, OK Air Show – October 2007

Denise Hill
Oklahoma City, OK
Hugo OK Air Show – October 2007

Pilots Chet Glenn and Joe Bunn
Hugo OK
Hugo, OK Air Show – October 2007

Donna Abbott
Hugo, OK
Hugo OK Air Show – October 2007

Gladys Sharp, Carla Rhodes and Samuel Rhodes
Hugo and Sawyer OK
Hugo, OK Air Show – October 2007

Ray and Ann Jordan
Hugo, OK
Hugo, OK Air Show – October 2007

Sheila Beard, Karla Cope, Jody Rawis, Kalyn, and Tristen
Hugo and Paris TX
Hugo, OK Air Show – October 2007

Lawan Wood
Hugo, OK
Hugo, OK Air Show – October 2007

Christina Capers, Angela Sparks, Debbie Park, Roy Lyles, Alyssa Wright and Ethan Sparks
Hugo, OK
Ilugo, OK Air Show – October 2007

Joe Webb
Hugo, OK
Hugo, OK Air Show – October 2007

Penny Harvey, Tom Nation, and Kacy Barlo
California and Soper, OK
Hugo, OK Air Show – October 2007

Amy Morris
Ft. Worth, TX
Hugo, OK Air Show – October 2007

Kay Fox, Nancy Wise, Howard Wise and Ruth Josey
Rockwall, TX, Arlington, TX and Oklahoma City, OK
Hugo, OK Air Show – October 2007

Private Instrument Pilot Danny Johnson
Plano, TX
I am in sales and promotions. My territory out of college was from Mississippi to Florida.
Now I own an agency and utilize my Baron for business flying!

Eddie and Chelsi Glenn
Hugo, OK
Hugo, Air Show – October 2007

Antonio Turner (Texarkana, TX). Dreamed of flying and is now a pilot.

David and Donna Webb (Atlanta, TX). Private Pilot. Loves flying.

Robert Jacobs (Denton, TX). Thinks flying is more exciting than working in an office.

Brian Davis (Durant, OK). Always wanted to be a pilot. Grew up around planes.

Jordan Powell (Wylie, TX). All of his family flies, so he wanted to learn to fly.

Andrew Lilley. Learning to fly has been a life long dream.

Brittan Kirk (Oklahoma City, OK). Family flew in the military, so he wanted to learn to fly.

Brenton Porter (Gainsville, TX). Always wanted to learn to fly.

Chris Glenn (Durant, OK). He says flying is his passion and his love and the only way to live.

Zachary Smith (Durant, OK). Says there is no other feeling in the world like flying.

Travis Smith (Greenville, TX). Starting flying at 18 and loves it.

Blayze Perkins (Grapevine, TX). Flies because he loves it.

Anthony Johnson (DeQueen, AR)

KT Granthan (Dallas, TX). Dad is a pilot. He has been around flying his whole life.

Tyler Dunn (Melissa, TX). Grew up flying with his dad and has always loved flying.

Austin McCann (Foothill Ranch, CA). Says he likes to go fast and has always loved flying.

Cole Cissell (Durant, OK). Flied for the Cessna 150s.

Jon Cobb (Lelina, TX). Loves flying because he likes to go fast.

Steven Kester (Sarasota, FL). Thinks flying is a way to do exciting and unusual things every day.

Chris Barthel (Oklahoma City, OK) Flying has been his dream since he was a child.

Paul Schad (Gainsville, TX). Grew up around an airport. He has been flying his whole life.

Steve Libick (Denton, TX). He always dreamed of learning to fly.

George Jacox (Durant, OK). Started flying in 1984.

Ben Kenagg (Cedar Park, TX). Dad took him flying and later paid for flying lessons.

1st Place Male Pilot Division – Walt, Idabel, Oklahoma. God Bless you and your family! We all miss you!

1st Solo Flight – Teresa (Idabel, Oklahoma).

1st Solo Flight – Cheryl (Idabel, Oklahoma)

1st Solo Flight – Teresa (Idabel, Oklahoma)

1st Solo Flight – Vicki (Commerce, Texas).

1st Solo Flight – Jeff (Mineola, Texas).

1st Solo Flight –Daryl (Broken Bow, Oklahoma).

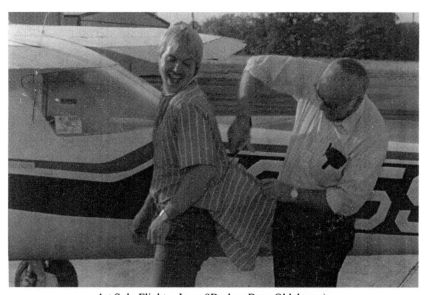

1st Solo Flight – Jerry 9Broken Bow, Oklahoma).

Susan cuts Jeff's shirt tail after his 1st Solo.

1st Solo Flight – Darrell (Idabel, Oklahoma).

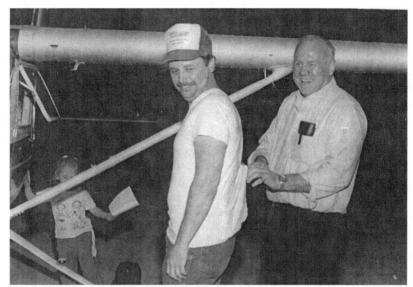

1st solo Flight – Daryl (Broken Bow, Oklahoma).

1st Solo Flight – Cheryl (Idabel, Oklahoma).

1st Solo Flight – Allen (Idabel, Oklahoma).

1st Solo Flight – Sue and Ronnie (Idabel,, Oklahoma).

1st Solo Flight – Jake (Bochito, Oklahoma).

1st Solo Flight – Cheryl (Idabel, Oklahoma)
Jones (Lindale, Texas).

1st Solo Flight – Mickey (Idabel, Oklahoma)

1st Solo Flight – David (Idabel, Oklahoma)

1st Solo Flight – Norman (Idabel, Oklahoma)

1st Solo Flight – Jack (Idabel, Oklahoma)

1st Solo Flight – Joe (Broken Bow, OK)

1st Solo Flight – Mark (Mt. Pleasant, Texas).

Max McLeod. Private Pilot. Flies for business.

Wes McMillon (DeKalb, TX). Private Pilot. Learned to fly in 1967 PVT 5EL.

Bill Murdock Jr. (Texarkana, TX). Private Pilot. Followed in dad's footsteps. Owns 1937 Taylor Model A.

Carl Staudridge Jr. (Texarkana, TX). Private-Instrument-Commercial. Flies to Nascar.

Mike Shewmaker (Texarkana, TX). Private Pilot. Loves the challenge of doing something different and new.

Rachael Shewmaker (Texarkana, TX). She started flying with her dad.

Jim Martin Jr. (Marietta, TX). Private Pilot. Third Generation Pilot. Grew up flying with his dad and mentor. Flies a RV-4.

Larry Weaver (Atlanta, TX). Private Pilot. Airport tramp since moving to Love Field after WWII at the age of 5 years.

Paul Tanner (Bonham, TX). Private Pilot.

Dr. Gusky (Gilmer, TX).

Private Pilot Austin Cude
Tulsa, OK
Lifelong dream to be a pilot!

Student Pilot Klass Banman with son, Celistino
Petty, TX

Private Pilot Justin Lee
Maud, TX

Private Pilot J.K. Weger
Paris, TX
It's the most fulfilling thing I do.

Private, Instrument, & Commercial Pilot Peter Harder Zacharias
Tigertown, TX

Private, Instrument, & Commercial Pilots Pete Zacharias & Henry Friesen
Tigertown, TX
Paris, TX

Josh Cantrell (Jacksonville, AR). Ratings: Private, Instrument. Josh files because there is nothing else like it in the world.

Joe Bunn (Hugo, OK). Joe is a private pilot and flies because his dad always wanted him to fly.

Bill Allan- Sulphur Springs, TX

Jesse Shipman (Honey Grove, TX). Ratings: Private, Instrument, Commercial. Jesse use his plane for business.

Cris Bookout (Texarkana, TX). Ratings: ATP, Multi-engine, Commercial, Single-engine, Instrument, Flight Instructor.

Richard Gumber (Texarkana, TX). He is a sport pilot and flies for fun.

ATP, A&P, Mechanic Inspection Authorization, Flight Instructor, Ground
Instructor, Leerjet, King Air 350 David W. Brown
Oklahoma City, Oklahoma

ATP, ASEL, ASES, AMEL, CFI, CFII, MLII, AGI, IGI Pilot Bob Newell
Yukon, OK
Wanted to hunt and fish in Alaska

Student Pilot Scott Hurley
Emory, TX
Something I wanted to do since the age of 16

Student Pilot Dennis Harwell
Telephone, TX

Private Pilot Phil Hale
Nacogdoches, TX
Pleasure then for business

Private Pilot John E. Hines
Points, TX

Private pilot Kenneth Taylor
Bonham, TX
For pleasure and relaxation

Private & Instrument Pilot Lou Peacock
Farmersville, TX

Private Pilot Matt Steward
Cumby, TX
Loved it from birth!

Private & Instrument Pilot Walter Hixson Magnolia, AR
Saves tons of time

Jake Harrell (Little Rock, AR). Ratings: Private, Instrument, Commercial. Jake always loved flying and thought it would be a fun career.

Hunter Byram (Searcy, AR). Ratings: Private, Instrument, Commercial, Multi-engine. Aviator major.

Trey McCully (Wylie, TX). Student Pilot. Loves flying because he loves the freedom.

Peter Wieler – right (Paris, TX). Private Pilot. Flying with a friend on a Sunday afternoon.

Wesley Bates, Emma Branton, Dona Branton, Ronnie Branton (Antlers, Oklahoma).

Jace Garrison (Ashdown, AR). Private Pilot.

Rick Shockley (Little Rock, Arkansas)
Flew for pleasure at first. Became very successful at network marketing in the Healthy
Chocolate Business (MXI Corp.) Rick enjoys traveling the U.S. sharing his successes in the
Healthy Chocolate Business. Flying saves him time.
Double Diamond Executive Healthy Chocolate Business

Ronnie Webb (Hobbs, New Mexico).
Flew for pleasure at first. Then, started flying to network marketing in the Healthy Chocolate Business (MXICorp.) Travels all over U.S. both private and commercial. Presidential Executive Double Diamond Healthy Chocolate Business

Private pilot Steve Stewart
DeQueen, AR
He wanted to fly all his life.

Private Pilot Grant Smith
DeQueen, AR

Private Instrument, Commercial, Multi Engine, CFi, CFii Pilot Trever Childs
DeQueen, AR

Private Instrument, Commercial, Multi Engine, CFi, CFii Pilot Trever Childs
Son Gabriel
DeQueen, AR

Private Instrument, Commercial, Cfi, CFii FAA Flight Examiner and Pilot Bill High
Hot Springs, AR

Private Instrument, Commercial, Pilot Joe Greer
DeQueen, AR

Private Instrument, Commercial – Multi – Engine Pilot Kent McClure
Atlanta, TX

Private, Instrument Pilot Dr. Mark Campbell with son Josh
Paris, TX

Chris Hill (Idabel, OK). Student Pilot.
He wanted to travel everywhere and be able to see the world.

Robert Timmer (Broken Bow, OK). Private Pilot.
He loves the view from above and loves being in control.
He just cannot get enough of it.

Private Pilot M.T. Schario (Marble Falls, TX). It's his fast transposrtation.

Multi engine, IFR Pilot Tom Shivey (Greenville, TX).

Private Pilot Bob F. Young (Mineola, TX). He saw WWII pilots in action.
Soloed in 1957. Was off for over 30 years. Now fly to get around faster than by car.

Multi engine, Commercial, Instrument Pilot Randy Garrison (Queen City, TX)
With Larry Ford. It's a family tradition and his father taught all his brothers and sisters to fly.

Commercial Pilot Roger Parks (Dallas, TX). His friend is a pilot and they started flying together. Pictured with Surry Shaffer

Multi engine, Commercial, Instrument Pilot Mike Anderson (Muskogee, OK). He loves airplanes.

Private, Instrument, Commercial, Multi-Engine, Cfi,
Cfii Pilot John Boyd (Little Rock, AR).

Multi Engine, ATP Pilot Major Wil Vessey USMC (Corpus Christi, TX) with wife Corie.
His family always was involved in aviation and he got hooked early on. He is currently a
flight instructor in the Marines and fly the T-45 and AV-813 as well as His piper Cherokee
PA-28-140. (his wife stuffs this one full of luggage and shopping.)

Private Pilots Jim and James Campbell (Icabel, OK). James was a high school football team mate of Bob Terry, Sr.

Private Pilot Dwayne Birdsong with wife Sharon (Idabel, OK).

Private, Instrument, Commercial, Multi-Engine Pilot Shawn Francis with son Chandler (Hugo, OK).

Student Pilot Chelsea Peacock (Honey Grove, TX)

Private, Instrument, Commercial, Pilot G.A. Merryworth (Lone Oak, TX)
It was a lifelong dream.

Private, Instrument, Multi-Engine Pilot Buck Hill with wife Natalie (Idabel, OK)

Private Pilot Timothy Glenn Chapman (Paris, TX)

Private Pilots brothers Brian and Brad Snider after 1st Solo Flight 12/16/07
Idabel, OK

Jimmie, Private Pilots Brian and Brad, Calen and Browning Snider
Idabel, OK

Private Pilots brothers Brian and Brad Snider with mother Gail and Brad's son Browning
Idabel, OK

Private Pilots Brian and Brad with father Billy and son Browning snider
Idabel, OK

Private Pilot Brad Snider with wife Ginny and daughter Brinlee and son Browning Idabel, OK

Private Pilot Brad Snider
Idabel, OK

ATP James Napurano and CFI, CFII, MEI Adam Koropsak
Addison, TX
For the love of aviation!

Commercial, CFII, A & P, IA Pilot Jim Folks
Greenville, TX
I wanted to fly since I was six.
I've been instructing since 1985 and I learned to fly in 1974.

Private Instrument Commercial CFI Pilot Sean Vaughan
Arkadelphia, AR
I always rode in the backseat with my dad and his flight instructor when I was 10. I thought his flight instructor had the coolest job in the world, so I eventually became a CFI myself.

Private Pilot Jenny Wei

Student Pilot Adam Kordsmeier
Conway, AR
Because I enjoy flying and want to make it a career.

Private Pilot Nathan Gerth
Arkadelphia, AR
Because I wanted to have a job that I would like to go to!

Private Instrument Commercial Pilot Jason Minchew
Arkadelphia, AR
Being stuck on the ground ruins my day.

Private Pilot Brian Grizzle
Arkadelphia, AR

Private Instrument Commercial CFI Pilot Nathan Bradshaw
I wanted to have a fun and exciting career!

Student Pilot Brandon Herring
It's Fun!

Private Instrument Commercial CFI Pilot Forrest Martin
Arkadelphia, AR
Flying was my first choice, as a child I would be working in the yard and hear an airplane go by, and I'd stop working and watch the airplane fly over until I couldn't see it anymore. This passion onkly intensified as I grew older.

Private Pilot Clay Phillips
I started flying for the view; everything looks so peaceful from the sky!

Private Instrument Commercial Pilot Andrew Williams
Clarendon, AR
The Girls!

Private Pilot Corey Hatfield
Cedarville, AR
It was always a dream of mine!

Private Instrument Commercial CFI Pilot Troy Hogue
Arkadelphia, AR
I just always loved the idea of flying and could not think of doing anything else.

Private Pilot Robert Stephenson
Arkadelphia, AR
I've always been amazed by airplanes and the sky.

Private Instrument Single Engine Pilot Bart Hause
Santa Ava, CA
For the love of flying!

Private Instrument Commercial ATP Pilot Conrad McEachern,
USAF, ROTC, SES, USAF 3 yrs, LA ANG 8 yrs/American
Airlines 28 years ATP Rating B707, B720, B727/B767, B757 with 20,000 hours
Dallas, TX

Private, Instrument Pilot Winn Harris
Lewisville, TX
I fly to work right now, but if I didn't I would find another reason to fly

Commercial Instrument Pilot Ben Mangan
Davenport, IA
I always thought it was neat, then when I was 17,
I took an introductory flight and the rest is history

Private Pilot James Finley
Greenville, TX
Because I love aviation and flying, for me it is relaxing and sets you free!

Student Pilot Ted Myers
Greenville, TX
I started flying due to a life long love of aviation!

Private Pilot Nick Russman
Merit, TX
I always wanted to learn how to fly and after going flying in a friend's mooney
I decided I was going to get my license.

Private Pilot Lyndol Erwin
Greenville, TX
I read a book called the "Purpose Driven Life" and found a way, and hope
To restore my childhood dream of flying, as I prepare to enter the missionary field.

Commercial Instrument Pilot Peter Zaccagnino
Flemington, NJ
Always wanted to fly and build and design aircraft.

Private Pilot Mark Hanson
Locust Grove, GA
I fly just for fun

Private Instrument Pilot Michael Luce
Greenville, TX
I have been interested in flying ever since I can remember, took ground school when I was 18, got married and never stepped into a plane until I was 39, now have been flying for 5 years and love it

Private Instrument Pilot Steven Schmillen
With Ina Schmillen, Alyda & Phil Ladenthin
Elkhorn, NE
I have wanted to fly ever since I was a kid.

Private, Instrument, Commercial, ATP, SEI, MEI Pilot Jeff Jennings
Oklahoma City, OK

CFI, CFII, MEI, SEI, ATP, Commercial Pilot Robert Terry
Yukon, OK

Private Pilot Bob DeMunck
Allen, TX
I fly for pleasure!

Private Pilot Kevin Groves
Allen, TX
I fly for the pleasure of it!

Private Pilot Larry C. Hughes
Pictured with Julie Vaughn, Youngest daughter and 1st Passenger
Alba, TX

Like most folks, I enjoyed watching airplanes fly. In high school, I read every book about flying in our small library. I dreamed of being a pilot for many years. I mowed a lawn across the street from a small airport and slipped in there on several occasions and flew imaginary trips in an old twin Cessna stored there. Later in life when my girls were out of high school I heard there was an instructor, Bob Terry, operating out of a local airport. I phoned him, took an introductory flight, and signed up for lessons on the spot. The uniqueness of flying an airplane still overwhelms me. I love the freedom of being in the air. I also enjoy offering flights to many near comers and love to hear the response of many after their very first flight.

A&P, Commercial, Single Engine, Multi Engine,
Instrument CFI Pilot Boyd L. Wheeler
Shreveport, LA
For a flying career!

Private Instrument, Commercial, Land & Sea Pilot Tim Mers
Haughton, LA
For the love of it. I like the convience, the challenge, and the beauty of it!

Dr. Mark Campbell (Paris, TX). NASA Medical Doctor.
Motivated him to become a private pilot. Private-Instrument Pilot.

Jason Mars (Mt. Pleasant, TX). Loves and thrill of high altitude. Student Pilot.

Rance Campbell (Mt. Pleasant, TX). Started flying as a way to get away. Student Pilot.

Philip Greenspan (Cambridge, MA). Loves flying because it is challenging.

Norman Haase (Ft. Towson, OK). Loves the challenge of high flight.

David Gillette, Rance Campbell, Jason Mars (Mt. Pleasant, TX). Friends that share the love of flying.

Student Pilot Rachael Meziere
Lavon, TX
Fell in love with this 3rd dimension and love to be in air

Private, AI, A&P Pilot Jim Carr with Dianne & Melody Carr
Winnsboro, TX
To be a mechanic you need to know how it flies inside and out

Student Pilot Ricky King
Winnsboro, TX

ATP, CFII, & Multi-Engine Pilot Bob Snow with daughter, Maegan
Rattan, OK

Private Pilot Ronnie Foster with wife, Amy
Winnsboro, TX
Always dreamed of being a commercial pilot

Student Pilot Robert Franklin with son, Harley
Greenville, TX
Because its fun and adventurous

ATP-CFII Pilot Jerry Richey
Private Pilot Brandi Richey
Pattonville, TX
Followed in my father's footsteps in aviation field

Private Pilot HLC Heath Roberts
Winnsboro, TX
Career

Private Pilot Ray Elgin
Winnsboro, TX

Private & Instrument Pilot Darren Couch
Celina, TX
Childhood dream!

Private Pilot Carl Elkins
Winnsboro, TX
My childhood "idol" Chuck Yeager was a pilot

Private Pilot Buzz Payne with friend Mike Sheeley
Big Sandy, TX
Fun and business

Commercial Pilot Jessie Shipman
Honey Grove, TX

Private, Instrument, Commercial, and Multi-Engine Pilot Jack Ashmore
Paris, TX
Introduced to flying at age 7 and been at it ever since

Private, Instrument, and Commercial Pilot Jacob Friesen with wife Jealene
Paris, TX
Have loved flying since age of 6 especially cross country to Mexico

Student Pilot Pete Buhler
Paris, TX
The Challenge

Commercial Pilot Gregg 'Tex" Roberts with wife Shae
Winnsboro, TX

Student Pilot Shae Roberts
Winnsboro, TX

Private Pilot Robert Suddeth
Mineola, TX
Private, Instrument, Commercial, and Multi-Engine Pilot Al Shuele with wife

Nancy
Austin, TX
USMC

Don Willingham (Brashear, Texas). Don retired from
the TX Highway Patrol and started a new hobby as a private pilot.

Rex Heminger and Kris Elkund (Dallas, Texas). Rex is an ATP. Kris is a student pilot.

Tom and Kim Knox (Paris, Texas). Tom always wanted to be a spray pilot. Ratings: Private-Instrument-Commercial-A&P.

Joe Kochick and Lindsey Oldham (Paris, Texas). Joe has always wanted to fly. Ratings: Private.

Larry Smith (Pagusa Springs, Colorado). Larry flies for the United States government.

Patrick Jenevein (Dallas, Texas). Patrick is a private pilot and loves flying because it saves time.

Mark Parsons and Dick Stephens (Richardson, Texas). Mark is a student pilot. He flies to reduce stress.

Sam Massey (Paris, Texas). Sam is a student pilot. He got his love for flying from his dad.

Zach Reeder (Mojave, California).
Zach is a private pilot. He first flew his dad's champ.

Gerald Carmack (Jasper, Texas). Gerald is a private pilot and loves to fly.

David Herbert, Mike Jenike, Kevin Herbert (San Angelo, Texas).
David started flying in 1974 and flies mostly for business.

William Brizzon (Greenville, Texas). William loves the fun and freedom of flying and
traveling.

Chad D. Parrott (Paris, Texas). Chad is a private pilot. He flies for enjoyment.

Bill Booth (Paris, Texas). Flying is Bill's professional dream. Ratings:
Private-Instrument-CFI-A&P.

C Olmsted and his neighbor Morgan Joslin (Sulphur Springs, Texas).
C is a private pilot.

Cody Stephens and Jimmy Smyers (Paris, Texas). Cody is an airline transport pilot for
Southwest Airlines. Jimmy is a commercial pilot.

ATP, MARTIN MEYER, ALBQUERORE, NM, ECLIPSE 500/F16

1ST SOLO 6-28-08, T.J. CREWS, SHIRT CUT OFF BY UNCLE JIM CREWS, CFI
IDABEL, OK

SPORT PILOTS: RUSTY MCCLAHAHAN, MARIN TOMULET FROM QUINLAN,
TEXAS AND STEVE LOPEZ FROM DALLAS, TEXAS CHALLENGE AND THE THRILL
OF MAN & MACHINE

SPORT & PRIVATE PILOT MARIN TOMULET

PRIVATE COMMERCIAL PILOT: STEVE DEAN, GILMER, TEXAS
JOINED THE SIR FORCE, FLEW IN VIETNUM

PRIVATE PILOT: MICHAEL G. COCO, PARIS, TEXAS
A LIFE LONG DREAM!! I WAITED UNTIL I WAS GROWN TO START (AGE 52)!!

COMMERICIAL FLIGHT INSTRUCTOR A&P: DONNIE ROYAL, QUINLAN, TEXAS
FATHER WAS A CROP DUSTER

PVT/INSTRUCTOR: ED MASON CLIFF GERBER, WESTLINN, OR
JUST HAD TO IT & MY GRANDMOTHER GAVE ME THE MONEY & SAID "ALL
MODERN MEN SHOULD KNOW HOW TO FLY"

PRIVATE PILOT: PETER FOOX, TYLER, TEXAS

PASSION SINCE I WAS A LITTLE BOY

COMMERCIAL INSTRUMENT SINGLE ENGINE LAND, MULTI ENGINE LAND, ATP:
VINNIE GRANDO, BOERNE, TEXAS
LIFE LONG DREAM!! WHEN I WAS A KID I LIVED UNDER AN APPROACH PATH
INTO RANDOLPH AFB. WHEN KIDS WERE PLAYING WITH TONKA TRUCKS I WAS
LOOKING UP AT THE SKY..DREAMING.

N8ZRV, ATP-B737ME, CPSE4HO70, CFIFW&HELO, CF11FW: RICHARD FREEMAN,
DENTON, TEXAS
HAD MY CALLING AT A EARLY AGE

Student Pilot Brandon Powell
Athens, TX
I've been around planes since 1985. Someday I would like to own a p40 warhawk. I just love planes.

Student Pilot Darrell Wright
Big Sandy, TX

ATP SMEL/COMMERCIAL SES & ROTORCRAFT/HELICOPTER, CFII,
(SMEL & HELICOPTER) A & P, IA/ Pilot Ray Burch--- Built 3 homebuilt Aircraft
Grand Saline, TX
Always loved airplanes. Moved in next door to a man who owned an aircraft in 1965. Went to
work for him as a line boy and have been at it ever since.

Private Pilot Troy Robinson
Quitman, TX 75783
To Get Away!

CFii-AGI, IGI, Mult & Single Engine Land, Instrument Pilot Larry Lowe
Seminole, OK
Love IT!

Private and Commercial Pilot Kent Walker
Idabel, OK
Pleasure of watching other pilots succeed.

Private Pilot Jim Martin Sr.
Over 300 Hours
Marietta, TX

Private Pilot Jim Martin Jr.
2nd Runner Up Private Pilot Under 200 Hours
Naples, TX
Nothing better to do, plain fun!

Private Pilot Jim Martin Sr. and Wife Annette
2nd Runner Up Over 300 Hours
Marietta, TX

Private Pilot Jim Martin Sr. and Son Private Pilot Jim Martin Jr.

Adult Sporty Student Pilot Aubrie Turner
3nd Runner UP, Atlanta, Tx Spot Landing
Texarkana, TX

Adult Sporty Student Pilot Aubrie Turner

Private, Instrument, Commercial Pilot Robert R. Hicks
Idabel, OK
Fun!

Private and Instrument Pilot Brent Bolen
Idabel, OK
Always wanted to fly when I was a kid. I like to see the world from a different view.

Private Pilots Noland Ashmore and Ruth Ann King
Bonham, TX
Expression of Freedom

Private Pilot Bubba Coston
Paris, TX
Soar with the Eagles!

Private Pilot Charles W. Davis
Paris, TX
I fly for the thrill and excitement!

Private Pilot Philip Whitaker
Paris, TX
I fly for the challenge!

Private Pilots Wilbur and Wilson Cox
Texarkana, AR
To get off the ground!

Private Pilot Walter DeVore
2nd Runner Up Private Pilot Over 300 Hours
Texarkana, TX

Private Instrument Commercial Helicopter Pilot Ray Hull
Waynoka, OK
I love Flying!

Private Instrument Commercial Wesley Rawle
with granddaughter Marliana Sander
Emory, TX
It looks like fun!

Private Pilot Brian Hunt
Winnsboro, TX

Private Pilot Brian Hunt and Family, (from left to right) Luci, Brian, Lydia, Mary and Private
Pilot Craig Kizer
Winnsboro, TX

ATP, CFII, MEII Pilot R L Ratliff and Private Multi-Engine Pilot Roy Truitt
Addison, TX
For business and pleasure!

Private Instrument Commercial Pilot Vernon Murphy with Pooh Wade
Texarkana, TX
Flying was a life time dream.

CFII Pilot Dennis Mathis
Greenville, TX
In early 50's, while on the farm, saw (and heard) a B-36 flying over. The dream started then.

Private Pilots Gary Gallandat and Bill Talutis
Echo Lake, TX
Flying was a life long dream!

Student Pilot Cody Roberts
Winnsboro, TX
Spot Landing Contest 2nd Runner Up Teenage Division Sept 15, 2007
In Atlanta, TX

Student Pilot Gregg Roberts
Winnsboro, TX
Spot Landing Contest 1st Runner Up Teenage Division Sept 15, 2007
In Atlanta, TX

Private Instrument Commercial Pilot Dean Smith
Broken Bow, OK
To further God's Work!

Future Pilot Nathan Smith (age 2 ½)
Broken Bow, OK
My future is flying! I love flying with my PaPa Dean Smith (above)

Private Pilot David Yturri
Dallas, TX
I always dreamed of flying and finally learned how after 9-11.

Private Instrument Commercial Pilot Tom Travis
Dallas, TX
I love the freedom of the flight!

Private Pilots James and Margaret Ashmore
Bonham, TX
We fly for the challenge!

Private Pilot Noland Ashmore with daughter and granddaughter
Bonham, TX
Save time traveling!

Private Sporty Pilot Norman Moorhead
Grand Champion Sporty Pilot Division
Bivins, TX

Private Instrument Commercial Pilot Steven A Davis
And wife Student Pilot Carolyn Davis
Texarkana, TX

Private, Instrument, Commercial, Pilot Charles Johnson and Son Carl Johnson
Barksdale AFB, LA
For the fun and freedom of being in the sky.
I always loved airplanes since I was very young.

Student Pilot Michael O Feavel, DDS
Benton, LA
It's exciting; challenging and I love to build my toys and
am interested in homebuilt aircraft.

Private, Instrument, Commercial, Single Engine, Multi Engine, ATP, CFI,
CFII Pilot James Walker
Shreveport, LA
Fell in love after my first flight at 7 years of age.

Instrument, Commercial, Multi Engine, Helicopter CFI Airplane-Helicopter
Pilot Gayle L. Robinson, Jr.
Marshall, TX
My father had a plane when I was young. I fell in love with flying and
decided in the 5th grade that flying is what I wanted to do!

Private Instrument Multi Engine Pilot Joe Provenza
Bossier City, LA

Private Instrument Pilot Richard Krouskop
Bellingham, WA
I was always interested in flying. My wife got tired of all the talk and no action and gave me and introductory lesson coupon for Christmas. Little did she know what she in for. Plane purchases and lots of cross country flights. We now commute regularly from Washington to Louisiana in my Debonair.

Private Instrument Pilot Brad Schmidt
Shreveport, LA
Because I wanted to get away!

Private Pilot Walter L. Cook Sr.
Bossier City, LA
As a kid, my father would take us to the airport on Sundays to see the aircraft landing and
Taking off. At 17 I joined the Air Force. Retired after 20 years. I guess I always wanted to fly.
Three years before I retired I got my private license.

PRIVATE INSTRUMENT COMMERICAL A&P, JIMMY SMYERS, PARIS, TEXAS

PRIVATE INSTRUMENT PILOT: RICHARD YAZELL, GILMER, TEXAS
I HAVE BEEN THRILL SEEKER SINCE I WAS A KID. FLYING IS A HEAVENLY
THRILL TO SOAR LIKE A EAGLE

Private Instrument Commercial Pilot Christ Hoss
Broken Bow, OK
1st Runner Up Commercial Pilot Division over 300 hours
Atlanta Spot Landing Contest September 15, 2007

Private Pilot Jim Henderson
Greenville, TX
I have wanted to fly since I was a very small child.
I did not get to until I was 50 years old!

Private Instrument Commercial Pilot LaRue Allen
2nd Runner UP, Atlanta, Tx Spot Landing
Over 300 Hours Commercial Division
Lindale, TX

Private Instrument Commercial Pilot Paul Lindsey
Quinlan, TX
Flying started as a hobby with my dad when I was sixteen and then lead to my career. I now fly
for UPS and I am only twenty five years old and
the first generation commercial pilot in my family.

ATP, Commercial, Instrument, Private, and A&P Pilot Boyd Proctor
Leesburg, TX
Fly for pleasure

Private, Multi-Engine Pilot Brian Proctor
Porterville, CA
Had a great chance to learn

281

Private Pilot Kevin Herrington
Honey Grove, TX
For Fun!

Student Pilot Jason Redus
Paris, TX
Going for commercial license

Private & Instrument Pilot Tom Noble
Winnsboro, TX
Pleasure

Commercial Pilot AJ Waters III with Pilot Dana Waters with Haylee Waters
Atlanta, TX

Tevis Pappas (Atlanta, TX). Ratings: Commercial Instrument, Flight Instructor, Multi-engine. He flies for business and pleasure.

Paul C. Smeltzer (Texarkana, TX). Sport pilot. He says that he started flying for the ladies.

Joe and Debbie Erbs (Enid, OK). Ratings:
Commercial Pilot, Instrument Pilot, Military Pilot.

Gene and Karen Pearcey (Durango, CO). Gene started flying at 15 and is now a private pilot.

Josh Jorgenson (Arkadelphia, AR). Ratings: Private,
Commercial, Instrument. Starting flying for his career.

Joe Don Burlsworth (Harrison, AR). Ratings: Private, Instrument, Commercial.

Paul Tumlison (Montecelo, AR). Ratings: Private, Instrument, Commercial. Paul has been interested in aviation his whole life.

John Knight (DeQueen, AR). Ratings: Private, Instrument

LaRue Allen (Grand Saline, TX). Ratings: Private, Instrument, Commercial.

Tim Parsons Jr. (Benton, AR). Tim is a student pilot and started flying for the career opportunities.

Nick Boyd (Arkadelphia, AR). Ratings: Private, Instrument, Commercial.

Jonathan Moss (Arkadelphia, AR). Ratings:
Private, Instrument, Commercial, Multi-engine

PRIVATE INSTRUMENT PILOT: RICHARD YAZELL, SHEADON WILLIAMS
(GRANDSON), TOMMY MOORE (SON-IN-LAW)

PRIVATE INSTRUMENT COMMERICAL MULIT A&P AI PILOT: JESSE LOFTIN WITH
DAUGHTER ALLISON

Student Pilot Jonathan Self
Campbell, TX
You can get to point A to point B a lot faster in an airplane than you can in a car! To Jonathan from all the pilots who appear in this book, We Salute You!! (At time of publishing this book, Jonathan was on active duty in Iraq.)

Private Pilot A L Self
Campbell, TX
As a child with my father and wanted to fly myself.

Private Pilot A L Self and wife Kathy
Campbell, TX

Student Pilot Jonathan Self With Family
A L Self, father, Kathy Self, mother, Kati Self, sister, and Clay, brother
Campbell, TX

Private, Instrument, Commercial, CFI Pilot Jim Crews
Millerton, OK
To become a flight instructor and the enjoyment of seeing others become pilots!

Sporty Pilot Roy and Betty Peevy - Granddaughter Keeli
Broken Bow, OK
A life long ambition as a child, I would watch an aircraft from the time I hear and locate it
until it left my vision, and at 62
years old I'm still amazed.

Private, Instrument Pilot Gary L. Rickey
Foreman, AR
Working with planes in the service, taking aviation courses in High School. Just the thrill and freedom. it's just in the blood!

Student Pilot Becky Wilemon
Shreveport, LA
It's just to much fun.

Zack Taylor (Texarkana, TX). Jill Caswell (Atlanta, TX).
Zack is a private pilot. Jill is a student pilot.

Lorenzo and Laurence Lasater (Greenville, TX). Laurence is a private pilote. Lorenzo uses his
plane for business.

Chelsea Peacock (Honey Grove, Texas)

Chelsea Peacock with dad, Toby (Honey Grove, Texas)

Chelsea Peacock (Honey Grove, Texas)

Chelsea Peacock with dad, Toby (Honey Grove, Texas)

Abram Rempel (Belize, Central America)

Terry Brooks with Wife, Susan (Paris, Texas)

Jennifer Jordan (Mount Vernon, Texas)

Dr. Mark Campbell and family (Parts, Texas)

Jennifer Jordan with fiancé, Chris Consola from Saltillo,
Texas (Mount Vernon, Texas)

Jennifer Jordan (Mount Vernon, Texas) with fiancé, Chris Consola (Saltillo, Texas)

Jennifer Jordan (Mount Vernon, Texas)

Tyler Briscoe (Ft. Towson, Oklahoma)

Skyler Burchinal (Paris, Texas)

Reily Andrews (Tyler, Texas)

Stephen Burgin (Lone Oak, Texas)

Stephen Burgin (Lone Oak, Texas)

Joe Vaughn (Broken Bow, Oklahoma)

Michael Russell (Paris, Texas)

Wylie Hockett (Petty, Texas)

Brandon Teignob, (Belize, South America)

Brandon Teignob (Belize, South America)

Rebecca Campbell (Paris, Texas)

Mark Campbell with daughter, Rebecca (Paris, Texas)

Emily Billings (Mount Vernon, Texas)

Emily Billings (Mount Vernon, Texas)

Anthony Croff (Paris, Texas)

Larry Billings and daughter, Emily (Mount Vernon, Texas)

Ricky Hevron with sons, Trevor and Devin (Honey Grove, Texas)

Tommy Hawks (Pittsburg, Texas)

Brandi Richey (Pattonville, Texas)

Tommy Hawks (Pittsburg, Texas)

Alan Russell Phillips (Broken Bow, Oklahoma)

Chris Methvin and family (Hugo, Oklahoma)

Ricky Hevron (Honey Grove, Texas)

Daniel Henry (Honey Grove, Texas)

Kent Walker and Gary Mulner (Idabel, Oklahoma)

Richard Miller (Hot Springs, Arkansas)

Ricky and Courtney Hevron (Honey Grove, Texas)

Glyn Thrash (Ashdown, Arkansas)

TJ Crews (Rome; Georgia)

Dough White and employees (Texarkana, Texas)

Mark Kenny Moore (Ashdown, Arkansas)

Mark Kenny Moore (Ashdown, Arkansas)

Jacob Morris (Idabel, Oklahoma)

Jacob Morris and family (Idabel, Oklahoma)

Nathan Lemmon (Atlanta, Texas)

Nathan Lemmon (Atlanta, Texas)

Chris H. (Idabel, Oklahoma)

Nathan Lemmon and David Webb (Atlanta, Texas)

Beth Nix (Mineola, Texas)

Everett Nix (Mineola, Texas)

Beth and Everett Nix (Mineola, Texas)

Candy and husband, Jackie Davidson (Blossom, Texas)

LaVergne, TN USA
06 January 2010

169068LV00001B/2/P